Cooking the Mediterranean Way

A Beginner's Cookbook for Wellness and Flavor

ANNA ROUX

TABLE OF CONTENTS

INTRODUCTION

Welcome to the Mediterranean Diet: A Journey to Health and Flavor

Welcome to the world of the Mediterranean diet, a culinary adventure that promises vibrant flavors and a path to improved well-being. Whether you're a seasoned food enthusiast or just beginning your exploration of healthy eating, you've embarked on a journey celebrating the Mediterranean region's rich traditions and bountiful cuisines.

Why the Mediterranean Diet?

The Mediterranean diet has gained global recognition for its exceptional health benefits and undeniable appeal to the senses. At its core, this dietary pattern is a celebration of fresh, whole foods that embrace the sun-kissed shores of the Mediterranean Sea. It's not just a diet; it's a way of life that has nourished generations and captured the hearts of food lovers worldwide.

A Rich Culinary Heritage

Imagine the azure waters of the Mediterranean, the sun-drenched landscapes of Greece, Italy, Spain, and the coasts of North Africa. These regions have been nurturing a culinary heritage for centuries. The Mediterranean diet reflects this heritage, where food isn't just sustenance; it's a celebration of life itself.

Heart Health at the Forefront

One of the standout features of the Mediterranean diet is its ability to promote heart health. The emphasis on healthy fats, particularly from olive oil, nuts, and fatty fish, reduces risk factors for heart disease. The Mediterranean diet is connected to fewer heart-related problems and longer lives for those who follow it.

Balanced and Sustainable

Unlike fad diets that advocate extreme restrictions or quick fixes, the Mediterranean diet is a sustainable approach to eating. It encourages balance and moderation rather than deprivation. With its focus on whole, minimally processed foods, it's a dietary pattern that can be enjoyed throughout life.

A Bounty of Nutrients

The Mediterranean diet is a treasure trove of essential nutrients. Fresh fruits and vegetables have minerals, vitamins, and antioxidants that are healthy for our bodies. Rich in omega-3 fatty acids, fish supports brain health and reduces inflammation. Legumes deliver plant-based protein and dietary fiber, promoting digestive health and satiety.

Culinary Pleasure

Food is meant to be enjoyed; the Mediterranean diet embraces this principle. The flavors are rich and diverse, with each ingredient playing a part in creating memorable meals. It's a diet that encourages savoring each bite, dining with loved ones, and relishing the pleasure of good food.

Scientific Validation

Decades of research have affirmed the health benefits of the Mediterranean diet. Scientific studies show it can help lower the chances of getting long-lasting diseases like heart disease, diabetes, and cancer. The Mediterranean diet is more than anecdotal; it's backed by extensive scientific evidence.

Environmental Stewardship

Aside from being good for your health, the Mediterranean diet supports sustainability and environmental care. Emphasizing local and seasonal produce, reducing red meat consumption, and incorporating plant-based ingredients, it's a diet that respects the planet as much as it nourishes the body.

A Journey Worth Taking

As you delve deeper into the pages of this cookbook, you'll uncover the secrets of Mediterranean cuisine. You'll learn how to harness the flavors of the Mediterranean to create dishes that not only tantalize your taste buds but also promote well-being.

The Mediterranean diet is more than a collection of recipes; it's an invitation to embrace a lifestyle that honors tradition, health and the pleasures of the table. It's a journey that can lead to a longer, healthier, and more flavorful life.

So, as you embark on this culinary adventure, savor the tastes, appreciate the history, and reap the benefits of the Mediterranean diet. It's a journey of a lifetime, and the rewards are boundless.

Principles of the Mediterranean Diet

At the heart of the Mediterranean diet are a few key principles that shape its delicious and healthful character:

1. **The Mediterranean diet has many fresh fruits and vegetables.** They provide a rainbow of flavors, essential nutrients, and antioxidants.
2. **Healthy Fats:** Olive oil takes center stage as a source of monounsaturated fats, promoting heart health and adding a luxurious touch to dishes.
3. **Lean Proteins:** Fish, seafood, poultry, and legumes provide ample protein without excessive saturated fats.
4. **Whole Grains:** Replace refined grains with quinoa, bulgur, and whole wheat pasta for added fiber and nutrients.
5. **Herbs and Spices:** Herbs like basil, rosemary, oregano, and spices like garlic and cumin, infuse dishes with bold flavors.
6. **Moderation:** Enjoying meals in moderation is a key principle. Savor every bite, and let your taste buds guide you.

Health Benefits

The Mediterranean diet is more than just a delicious way to eat—it's a powerful tool for enhancing your well-being. Studies have shown that it may:

- Lower the chance of getting heart disease and stroke.
- Improve cholesterol levels
- It helps control blood sugar and lowers the risk of type 2 diabetes.
- Promote weight management
- Promote brain well-being and lower the chance of cognitive decline.
- We have many different vitamins, minerals, and antioxidants for you.

Getting Started

This cookbook will explore the flavors and recipes that define the Mediterranean diet. You'll discover how to create mouthwatering dishes that are good for your health and a joy to prepare and share with loved ones.

So, whether you're here to embrace a new way of eating or to deepen your culinary expertise, we invite you to savor the Mediterranean diet—a journey of health and flavor that will delight your taste buds and nourish your body and soul.

CHAPTER 1:
THE MEDITERRANEAN PANTRY

Stocking Your Kitchen: Essential Ingredients

A well-stocked kitchen is essential before you embark on your culinary journey through the Mediterranean diet. The Mediterranean way of eating revolves around fresh, high-quality ingredients that form the foundation of delicious and healthy meals. In this chapter, we'll explore the essential ingredients that will bring the flavors of the Mediterranean to your home.

1. Olive Oil: Liquid Gold of the Mediterranean

Olive oil is a very important part of Mediterranean cooking. It's not just a cooking oil; it's a precious elixir that infuses dishes with a rich, fruity aroma and a delicate, nutty flavor. Look for extra-virgin olive oil, as it's less processed and retains more of the olive's natural goodness. Use it for sautéing, drizzling over salads, and dipping with crusty bread.

2. Vinegar: A Symphony of Flavors

Vinegar is essential for adding zing to your Mediterranean dishes. Balsamic, red, and white wine vinegar are commonly used. They enhance salad dressings, marinades, and sauces. Experiment with different tablespoons of vinegar to discover your favorite flavor combinations.

3. Whole Grains and Pasta

Whole grains are a hearty and nutritious staple of the Mediterranean diet. Options like bulgur, quinoa, whole wheat couscous, and brown rice are perfect for pilafs, salads, and side dishes. Traditional pasta made from durum wheat is also prevalent, used in classic dishes like spaghetti with tomato sauce or pasta primavera.

4. Fresh Herbs and Spices

Fresh herbs and spices stand out in Mediterranean cuisine, elevating dishes with their aromatic profiles. Basil, oregano, rosemary, thyme, and mint are examples. Keep a small herb garden or potted herbs on your kitchen windowsill for easy access to these flavorful additions. Don't forget to explore the world of spices like cumin, coriander, and paprika to add depth and character to your meals.

5. Fruits and Vegetables

The Mediterranean diet celebrates the vibrant colors and flavors of fruits and vegetables. Stock your kitchen with fresh produce, including tomatoes, cucumbers, bell peppers, eggplants, zucchini, lemons, and oranges. These ingredients form the basis of salads, stews, and side dishes, contributing to the diet's healthful reputation.

6. Nuts and Seeds

Nuts and seeds provide a satisfying crunch and a wealth of nutrients. Mediterranean cuisine often uses almonds, walnuts, pistachios, and pine nuts. Sprinkle them over salads, add them to couscous dishes, or use them as a garnish for desserts. Sesame seeds and tahini (sesame paste) are also staples, essential for making dishes like hummus and tahini sauce.

7. Seafood and Lean Proteins

Seafood is a significant protein source in the Mediterranean diet. Incorporate a variety of fish, such as salmon, sardines, mackerel, and tuna, into your meals. Chicken and turkey, which are types of lean proteins, are also part of the category. Opt for fresh, sustainably sourced seafood whenever possible.

8. Dairy and Dairy Alternatives

Dairy products like yogurt and cheese are part of the Mediterranean diet, but many traditional recipes also feature dairy alternatives like plant-based yogurt or nut-based cheeses. Greek yogurt is particularly popular for its creaminess and versatility.

These essential ingredients are the building blocks of Mediterranean cuisine. As you explore the recipes in this cookbook, you'll become intimately familiar with these elements, using them to create delicious and nourishing dishes. So, let's roll up our sleeves, stock our kitchens, and embark on a flavorful journey through the Mediterranean diet!

CHAPTER 2: MEDITERRANEAN BREAKFASTS

MEDITERRANEAN SCRAMBLE

Prep Time: 10 minutes | **Cook Time:** 10 minutes | **Servings:** 2

Ingredients:

- 4 large eggs
- 2 tablespoons extra-virgin olive oil
- 1/2 small red onion, finely chopped
- 1/2 red bell pepper, diced
- 1/2 yellow bell pepper, diced
- 1 cup cherry tomatoes, halved
- 1/2 cup baby spinach leaves
- 1/4 cup crumbled feta cheese
- 2 tablespoons chopped fresh parsley
- Salt and pepper to taste

Instructions:

1. **Prepare Your Ingredients:** Chop the red onion, red and yellow bell peppers, cherry tomatoes, and fresh parsley. Crumble the feta cheese.
2. **Beat the Eggs:** Break them into a bowl, add some salt and pepper, and mix them using a whisk until thoroughly blended. Put to the side.
3. **Sauté the Vegetables:** Heat the olive oil in a non-stick skillet over medium-high heat. Add the chopped red onion and sauté for 2 minutes | until it softens.

4. **Add the Bell Peppers:** Add the diced red and yellow bell peppers to the skillet with the onions. Sauté for an additional 3-4 minutes | until the peppers become tender.
5. **Tomatoes and Spinach:** Toss the halved cherry tomatoes and baby spinach leaves. Cook for 2 minutes | until the spinach wilts and the tomatoes soften slightly.
6. **Scramble the Eggs:** Pour the whisked eggs over the sautéed vegetables in the skillet. Blend persistently with a spatula until the eggs begin to set but are still marginally runny.
7. **Add Feta and Parsley:** Sprinkle the crumbled feta cheese and chopped fresh parsley over the partially set eggs. Continue to stir gently until the eggs are fully cooked but still moist.
8. **Season to Taste:** Taste the scramble and season with additional salt and pepper if needed.
9. **Serve:** Divide the Mediterranean Scramble between two plates. Garnish with a bit more fresh parsley if desired.

Nutrition Information (per serving):

- Calories: 295 kcal
- Protein: 11g
- Carbohydrates: 9g
- Dietary Fiber: 2g
- Sugars: 4g
- Fat: 24g
- Saturated Fat: 6g
- Cholesterol: 356mg
- Sodium: 360mg
- Potassium: 395mg

SCRAMBLED EGG TACOS

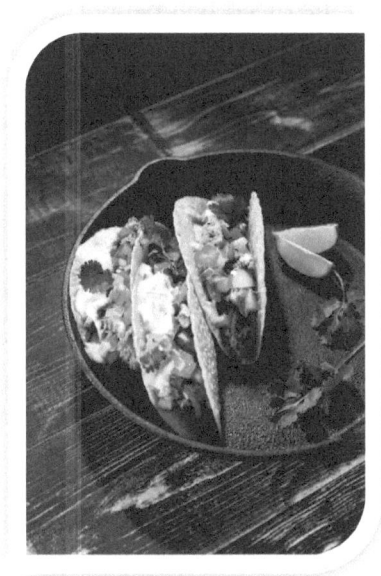

Prep Time: 10 minutes | **Cook Time:** 10 minutes | **Servings:** 2

Ingredients:

- 4 large eggs
- 1/4 cup milk
- 1/2 cup of diced bell peppers, which can be any color.
- 1/4 cup diced red onion
- 1/2 cup shredded cheddar cheese
- 4 small flour tortillas
- 2 tablespoons butter or cooking oil
- Salt and pepper to taste
- Optional toppings: salsa, diced tomatoes, chopped fresh cilantro, sour cream, avocado slices

Instructions:

1. **Prepare Your Ingredients:** Dice the bell peppers and red onion. Shred the cheddar cheese. If you're using any optional toppings, prepare them as well.

11

2. **Whisk the Eggs:** Break the chicken eggs into a bowl, pour in the milk, and add a little salt and pepper. Whisk until well combined.
3. **Sauté Vegetables:** Heat a large skillet over medium-high heat and add the butter or cooking oil. Once hot, add the diced bell peppers and red onion. Sauté for about 3-4 minutes | until they start to soften.
4. **Scramble Eggs:** Push the sautéed vegetables to one side of the skillet and pour the whisked eggs into the other. Let them cook for a moment without stirring, then gently scramble them with a spatula as they start to set.
5. **Add Cheese:** When the eggs are almost fully cooked but still slightly runny, sprinkle the shredded cheddar cheese over the top. Stir until the cheese is melted and the eggs are fully cooked.
6. **Warm Tortillas:** While cooking eggs, warm the flour tortillas in a dry skillet or microwave for about 20 seconds.
7. **Assemble Tacos:** Divide the scrambled eggs evenly among the warm tortillas. Add any optional toppings, such as salsa, diced tomatoes, chopped fresh cilantro, sour cream, or avocado slices.
8. **Fold and Serve:** Fold the tortillas in half to form tacos. Serve immediately.

Nutrition Information (per serving, without optional toppings):

- Calories: 358 kcal
- Protein: 18g
- Carbohydrates: 19g
- Dietary Fiber: 2g
- Sugars: 2g
- Fat: 23g
- Saturated Fat: 10g
- Cholesterol: 381mg
- Sodium: 433mg
- Potassium: 284mg

PAN CON TOMATE (TOMATO BREAD)

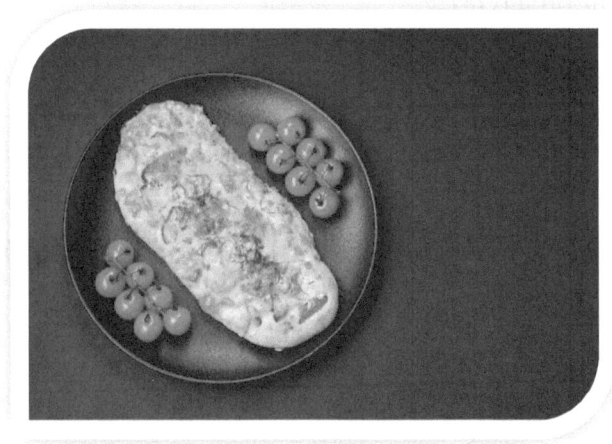

Prep Time: 10 minutes | **Cook Time:** 5 minutes | **Servings:** 4

Ingredients:

- 4 slices of rustic bread (baguette or ciabatta work well)
- 2 ripe tomatoes
- 2 cloves garlic, peeled
- Extra-virgin olive oil
- Salt to taste
- Freshly ground black pepper
- Optional toppings: Serrano ham, Manchego cheese, or fresh basil leaves

Instructions:

1. **Toast the Bread:** Preheat your oven's broiler or toaster. Place the bread slices on a baking sheet and toast them until golden brown, turning once to toast both sides evenly. Keep a close eye on them to prevent burning. Or, you can heat the bread in a toaster or on a grill.
2. **Prepare the Tomatoes:** Cut the ripe tomatoes in half. Rub the cut side of the tomatoes over the toasted bread slices. The juicy flesh of the tomato should be pressed onto the bread, creating a natural tomato sauce.
3. **Garlic Infusion:** Rub gently rub the peeled garlic cloves over the tomato-covered bread. The friction will release the garlic's aroma and add a subtle garlicky flavor.

13

4. **Drizzle with Olive Oil:** Generously drizzle extra-virgin olive oil over each slice of tomato-covered bread. This not only adds flavor but also moistens the bread.
5. **Season:** Put some salt and pepper on the Pan Con Tomate. Change the flavorings according to your preference.
6. **Optional Toppings:** If desired, top the Pan Con Tomate with slices of Serrano ham, thin shavings of Manchego cheese, or fresh basil leaves. These additions complement the dish beautifully.
7. **Serve:** Pan Con Tomate is best served immediately while the bread is still warm and the flavors are fresh.

Nutrition Information (per serving, without optional toppings):

- Calories: 180 kcal
- Protein: 4g
- Carbohydrates: 28g
- Dietary Fiber: 2g
- Sugars: 2g
- Fat: 6g
- Saturated Fat: 1g
- Cholesterol: 0mg
- Sodium: 270mg
- Potassium: 160mg

SWEET POTATO HASH WITH EGGS

Prep Time: 15 minutes | **Cook Time:** 20 minutes | **Servings:** 2

Ingredients:

- Two medium sweet potatoes were peeled and cut into small cubes.
- 1/2 onion, finely chopped
- 1 red bell pepper, diced
- 2 cloves garlic, minced
- 2 tablespoons olive oil
- 1 teaspoon smoked paprika
- 1/2 teaspoon ground cumin
- Salt and pepper to taste
- 4 large eggs
- Add fresh parsley or cilantro on top (if you want to).
- Hot sauce or salsa (optional for serving)

Instructions:

1. **Prepare Sweet Potatoes:** Peel and dice the sweet potatoes into small, uniform cubes.

2. **Sauté Onions and Garlic:** Heat the olive oil over medium-high heat in a large skillet. Add the chopped onions and minced garlic. Sauté for about 2-3 minutes | until they become fragrant and translucent.
3. **Add Sweet Potatoes:** Add the diced sweet potatoes to the skillet. Spread them out in a single layer. Let them cook without stirring for a few minutes, allowing one side to brown slightly. Then, stir and cook for another 8-10 minutes | or until the sweet potatoes are tender and have a crispy exterior.
4. **Season and Spice:** Season the sweet potatoes with smoked paprika, ground cumin, salt, and pepper. Stir well to coat all the cubes evenly. Continue cooking for 2-3 minutes, allowing the spices to infuse into the sweet potatoes.
5. **Add Red Bell Pepper:** Toss in the diced red bell pepper and cook for 2-3 minutes | until the pepper softens slightly but retains a bit of crunch.
6. **Create Wells for Eggs:** Use a spoon to create four small wells or indentations in the sweet potato hash.
7. **Crack Eggs:** Carefully crack an egg into each will lower the temperature, put a lid on the skillet, and let the eggs cook for 5-7 minutes | until the whites are set but the yolks are still slightly runny. If you prefer firmer yolks, cook for an additional 1-2 minutes.
8. **Garnish and Serve:** Once the eggs are cooked to your liking, garnish the sweet potato hash with chopped fresh parsley or cilantro. Optionally, serve with hot sauce or salsa on the side for added flavor and heat.
9. **Serve Hot:** Carefully scoop portions of the sweet potato hash with eggs onto plates and serve immediately while it's hot.

Nutrition Information (per serving):

- Calories: 310 kcal
- Protein: 10g
- Carbohydrates: 34g
- Dietary Fiber: 6g
- Sugars: 8g
- Fat: 16g
- Saturated Fat: 3g
- Cholesterol: 186mg
- Sodium: 196mg
- Potassium: 753mg

GREEK OMELETTE WITH ZUCCHINI AND MINT (CRETE)

Prep Time: 10 minutes | **Cook Time:** 15 minutes | **Servings:** 2

Ingredients:

- 4 large eggs
- 1 medium zucchini, thinly sliced
- 1/2 red onion, finely chopped
- 2 tablespoons fresh mint leaves, chopped
- 2 tablespoons extra-virgin olive oil
- Salt and pepper to taste
- Feta cheese, crumbled, for garnish (optional)
- Fresh mint leaves, for garnish (optional)

Instructions:

1. **Prepare Your Ingredients:** Cut the zucchini into thin slices, chop the red onion into small pieces, and chop the fresh mint leaves. Crumble the feta cheese if you're using it as a garnish.
2. **Sauté Zucchini and Onion:** Heat the olive oil in a non-stick skillet over medium-high heat. Add the chopped red onion and sliced zucchini. Sauté for about 5-7 minutes, or until the zucchini becomes tender and slightly golden.

17

3. **Season and Add Mint:** Put salt and pepper on the zucchini and onion mixture. Add the fresh mint leaves and cook for 1-2 minutes | so that the mint can give a nice smell to the mixture. Remove the mixture from the skillet and set it aside.
4. **Whisk Eggs:** In a bowl, whisk the eggs until they are well beaten. Add salt and pepper to the eggs at your discretion.
5. **Cook Omelette:** Return the skillet to the heat, and add more olive oil if needed. Pour the beaten eggs into the skillet, spreading them evenly. Allow the eggs to cook undisturbed for a few minutes | until the edges start to set.
6. **Add Zucchini Mixture:** Spoon the sautéed zucchini, onion, and mint mixture evenly over one half of the omelet.
7. **Fold and Serve:** Carefully fold the other half of the omelet over the zucchini mixture to create a half-moon shape. Cook for 2-3 minutes | until the eggs are fully set but slightly moist inside.
8. **Garnish and Serve:** Transfer the Greek Omelette with Zucchini and Mint to a serving plate. If desired, garnish with crumbled feta cheese and additional fresh mint leaves.
9. **Serve Hot:** Slice the omelet into wedges and serve hot.

Nutrition Information (per serving, without optional garnishes):

- Calories: 217 kcal
- Protein: 12g
- Carbohydrates: 7g
- Dietary Fiber: 2g
- Sugars: 3g
- Fat: 15g
- Saturated Fat: 3g
- Cholesterol: 327mg
- Sodium: 87mg
- Potassium: 442mg

SHEET PAN EGG TACOS

Prep Time: 15 minutes | **Cook Time:** 15 minutes | **Servings:** 4

Ingredients:

- 8 large eggs
- 4 small flour tortillas
- 1 cup diced bell peppers (any color)
- 1 cup diced red onion
- 1 cup diced tomatoes
- 1 cup shredded cheddar cheese
- 1 tablespoon olive oil
- Salt and pepper to taste
- Fresh cilantro leaves for garnish (optional)
- Salsa or hot sauce for serving (optional)

Instructions:

1. **First,** turn on your oven and set it to the temperature of 375°F (190°C).
2. **Prepare Sheet Pan:** Put parchment paper or a cooking spray on a sheet pan.

3. **Sauté Vegetables:** Heat the olive oil over medium-high heat in a large skillet. Add the diced bell peppers and red onion. Sauté for about 3-4 minutes | until they start to soften.
4. **Whisk Eggs:** In a bowl, whisk the eggs until well beaten. Sprinkle some salt and pepper to make it taste better.
5. **Add Eggs to Sheet Pan:** Pour the beaten eggs onto the prepared sheet pan. Spread them out evenly.
6. **Add Vegetables and Cheese:** Sprinkle the sautéed bell peppers and red onion over the eggs. Add the diced tomatoes and shredded cheddar cheese.
7. **Bake:** Place the sheet pan in the oven and bake for approximately 12-15 minutes, or until the eggs are set and the cheese is melted.
8. **Warm Tortillas:** While the eggs are baking, warm the flour tortillas in the oven for a few minutes | or in a dry skillet until they are heated through.
9. **Assemble Tacos:** Remove the sheet pan from the oven once the eggs are cooked. Cut the egg mixture into quarters.
10. **Fill Tortillas:** Place each quarter of the egg mixture onto a tortilla. Fold the tortilla over the eggs to create a taco.
11. **Garnish:** Garnish the Sheet Pan Egg Tacos with fresh cilantro leaves if desired.
12. **Serve:** Serve the tacos immediately with salsa or hot sauce on the side for those who prefer extra flavor and heat.

Nutrition Information (per serving, 1 taco):

- Calories: 315 kcal
- Protein: 17g
- Carbohydrates: 21g
- Dietary Fiber: 2g
- Sugars: 4g
- Fat: 18g
- Saturated Fat: 6g
- Cholesterol: 371mg
- Sodium: 433mg
- Potassium: 333mg

SPINACH AND GOAT CHEESE QUICHE

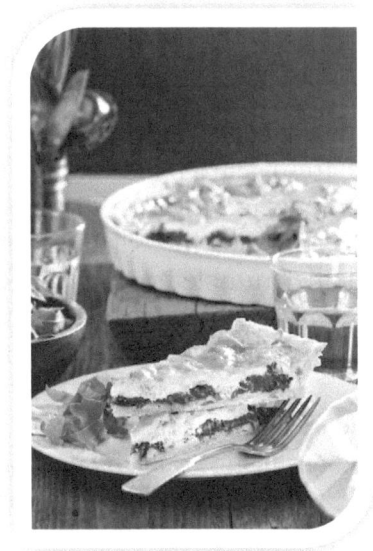

Prep Time: 20 minutes | **Cook Time:** 40 minutes | **Servings:** 6

Ingredients:

- 1 pie crust (store-bought or homemade)
- 6 large eggs
- 1 cup fresh spinach, chopped
- 1/2 cup crumbled goat cheese
- 1/2 cup milk (any type, such as whole, skim, or almond milk)
- 1/2 cup heavy cream
- 1/4 cup grated Parmesan cheese
- 1/2 small onion, finely chopped
- 1 clove garlic, minced
- 1/2 teaspoon dried thyme
- Salt and pepper to taste
- Olive oil for sautéing

Instructions:

1. **Preheat Oven:** Turn on your oven and set it to 375°F (190°C). Put the pie crust in a 9-inch (23 cm) pie dish and leave it there.
2. **Sauté Onion and Garlic:** Put some of your favorite olive oil in a pan and warm it on medium heat. Add the onion that has been finely cut into small pieces and the garlic that has been crushed into a very fine texture. Sauté for about 2-3 minutes | until they become fragrant and translucent. Remove from heat and set aside.
3. **Prepare Spinach:** Chop the fresh spinach into smaller pieces.
4. **Whisk Egg Mixture:** In a bowl, whisk together the eggs, milk, heavy cream, and grated Parmesan cheese; mix dried thyme, salt, and pepper until evenly distributed.
5. **Layer Ingredients:** Sprinkle the crumbled goat cheese evenly over the bottom of the pie crust. Next, add the sautéed onion, garlic and chopped spinach.
6. **Pour Egg Mixture:** Carefully pour the egg mixture over the ingredients in the pie crust.
7. **Cook:** Put the quiche in the oven and cook for about 35-40 minutes | until the top is golden brown and the middle is firm. You can check if the quiche is cooked by poking a knife or toothpick in the middle. If it comes out clean, then it is ready.
8. **Cool and Serve:** Allow the quiche to cool for a few minutes | before slicing and serving. You can eat it when it's warm or when it's not too hot or cold.

Nutrition Information (per serving, assuming 6 servings):

- Calories: 316 kcal
- Protein: 12g
- Carbohydrates: 17g
- Dietary Fiber: 1g
- Sugars: 1g
- Fat: 22g
- Saturated Fat: 11g
- Cholesterol: 207mg
- Sodium: 405mg
- Potassium: 224mg

SPINACH AND RICOTTA FRITTATA

Prep Time: 15 minutes | **Cook Time:** 20 minutes | **Servings:** 4

Ingredients:

- 6 large eggs
- 1 cup fresh spinach, chopped
- 1/2 cup ricotta cheese
- 1/2 cup grated Parmesan cheese
- 1/2 small onion, finely chopped
- 1 clove garlic, minced
- 1/2 teaspoon dried oregano
- Salt and pepper to taste
- Olive oil for sautéing

Instructions:

1. **Preheat Oven:** Preheat your oven to 350°F (175°C).
2. **Sauté Onion and Garlic:** Heat olive oil over medium heat in an oven-safe skillet. Put the finely cut onion and crushed garlic in. Sauté for about 2-3 minutes | until they become fragrant and translucent.
3. **Add Spinach:** Add the chopped fresh spinach to the skillet and sauté for 2-3 minutes | until the spinach wilts and any excess moisture evaporates. Remove from heat and set aside.

4. **Whisk Egg Mixture:** In a bowl, whisk together the eggs, ricotta cheese, grated Parmesan cheese, dried oregano, salt, and pepper until well combined.
5. **Combine Ingredients:** Stir the sautéed spinach mixture into the egg mixture, ensuring the ingredients are evenly distributed.
6. **Cook Frittata:** Return the skillet to the stove over medium heat. If you need to, you can add a little more olive oil. Put the mix of egg and spinach into the frying pan and cook it for about 3-4 minutes | or until the edges solidify.
7. **Transfer to Oven:** Put the skillet in the oven that has been heated beforehand and bake for about 12-15 minutes | until the frittata in the middle is fully cooked and slightly bigger.
8. **Cool and Serve:** Allow the frittata to cool briefly before slicing and serving. It can be heated up or left as is.

Nutrition Information (per serving, assuming 4 servings):

- Calories: 220 kcal
- Protein: 15g
- Carbohydrates: 3g
- Dietary Fiber: 1g
- Sugars: 1g
- Fat: 16g
- Saturated Fat: 7g
- Cholesterol: 279mg
- Sodium: 342mg
- Potassium: 232mg

TRADITIONAL ITALIAN BISCOTTI

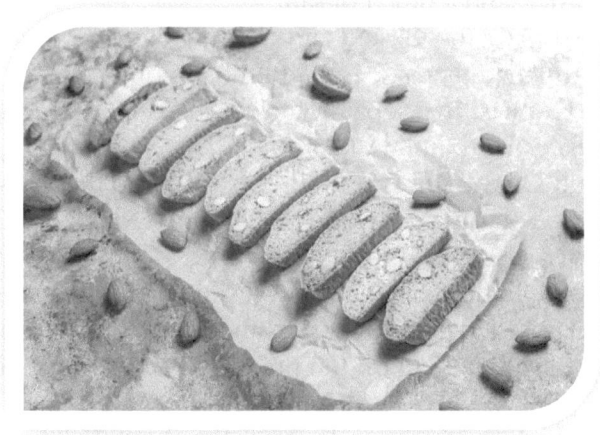

Prep Time: 20 minutes | **Cook Time:** 50 minutes | **Servings:** Approximately 24 biscotti

Ingredients:

- 2 cups all-purpose flour
- 1 cup granulated sugar
- 1/2 cup unsalted almonds, whole or sliced
- 1/2 cup unsalted pistachios, roughly chopped
- 2 large eggs
- 2 egg yolks
- 1 teaspoon baking powder
- 1/2 teaspoon almond extract
- 1/2 teaspoon vanilla extract
- Zest of 1 lemon or orange
- Pinch of salt

Instructions:

1. **Preheat Oven:** Turn your oven on and set it to 350 degrees Fahrenheit (or 175 degrees Celsius). Put parchment paper or a silicone baking mat on a baking sheet.
2. **Toast Nuts (Optional):** If using whole almonds, you can toast them for added flavor. Place the almonds on a baking sheet and cook them in the oven for around 8-10

minutes | until they smell good and turn slightly brown. Remove from the oven and let them cool before roughly chopping them.

3. **Mix Dry Ingredients:** In a bowl, whisk together the all-purpose flour, granulated sugar, baking powder, and a pinch of salt.
4. **Add Nuts and Zest:** Add the toasted almonds (or sliced almonds) and chopped pistachios to the dry ingredients. Also, add the lemon or orange zest. Mix everything.
5. **Whisk Eggs and Extracts:** In a separate bowl, whisk the eggs, egg yolks, almond extract, and vanilla extract until well combined.
6. **Combine Wet and Dry Mixtures:** Put the wet stuff into the dry stuff and mix it until it turns into a dough. You can gently knead the dough with a wooden spoon or your hands.
7. **Shape the Dough:** Split the dough into two even parts. On a flat surface, sprinkle a bit of flour. Then, shape each part into a thin and long-form, around 12 inches in length and 2 inches in width. Put them on the prepared baking sheet; leave some space between them.
8. **First Bake:** Bake the biscotti logs in the oven for about 25-30 minutes | or until they are lightly golden and firm to the touch.
9. **Cool Slightly:** Take the biscotti out of the oven and cool on the baking sheet for approximately 10 minutes. Turn the oven heat to 325 degrees Fahrenheit (160 degrees Celsius).
10. **Slice Biscotti:** Using a sharp knife, slice the biscotti logs diagonally into 1/2-inch thick pieces. Place the slices back on the baking sheet and cut sides up.
11. **Second Bake:** Put the biscotti back in the oven and cook for 15-20 minutes | or until they turn golden and crispy. You can turn them over before baking to ensure they brown evenly.
12. **Cool Completely:** Take the biscotti out of the oven and cool on a metal grid.
13. **Serve:** Serve these Traditional Italian Biscotti with your favorite coffee or tea.

Nutrition Information (per biscotti, approximate):

- Calories: 120 kcal
- Protein: 2.5g
- Carbohydrates: 15g
- Dietary Fiber: 1g
- Sugars: 8g
- Fat: 5.5g
- Saturated Fat: 0.5g
- Cholesterol: 27mg
- Sodium: 2mg
- Potassium: 64mg

AVOCADO TOAST WITH SMOKED SALMON, CAPERS, AND FRESH DILL

Prep Time: 10 minutes | **Cook Time:** None | **Servings:** 2

Ingredients:

- 2 slices of whole-grain bread (or bread of your choice)
- 1 ripe avocado
- 4 ounces (about 113 grams) smoked salmon
- 2 tablespoons capers, drained
- Fresh dill sprigs for garnish
- Lemon wedges for serving (optional)
- Salt and black pepper to taste
- Extra-virgin olive oil for drizzling (optional)

Instructions:

1. **Toast-Bread (Optional):** If you prefer your toast to be warm and slightly crispy, you can toast the slices of bread in a toaster or on a stovetop grill until they reach your desired level of crispiness.
2. **Prepare Avocado:** Cut the ripe avocado in half and remove the pit. Put the fruit or vegetable inside a bowl. To smooth the avocado, use a fork and keep mashing it until it reaches the desired creaminess. You can keep it a bit bumpy or make it even.

27

3. **Assemble Avocado Toast:** Spread the mashed avocado evenly over the toasted bread slices.
4. **Add Smoked Salmon:** Layer the smoked salmon over the mashed avocado.
5. **Sprinkle Capers:** Sprinkle the drained capers over the smoked salmon.
6. **Season:** Season the toast with a pinch of salt and a grind of black pepper to taste. Be mindful of the salt, as smoked salmon and capers are naturally salty.
7. **Garnish with Dill:** Garnish the Avocado Toast with fresh dill sprigs for a burst of flavor and a beautiful presentation.
8. **Optional Drizzle:** Drizzle a bit of extra-virgin olive oil over the top for added richness.
9. **Serve:** Serve the Avocado Toast with Smoked Salmon, Fresh Dill, and Capers immediately. You can also add lemon slices to the side of the dish for a tangy flavor.

Nutrition Information (per serving, 1 slice of toast):

- Calories: 278 kcal
- Protein: 16g
- Carbohydrates: 19g
- Dietary Fiber: 6g
- Sugars: 2g
- Fat: 16g
- Saturated Fat: 3g
- Cholesterol: 14mg
- Sodium: 992mg
- Potassium: 686mg

BREAKFAST TORTA WITH JAM

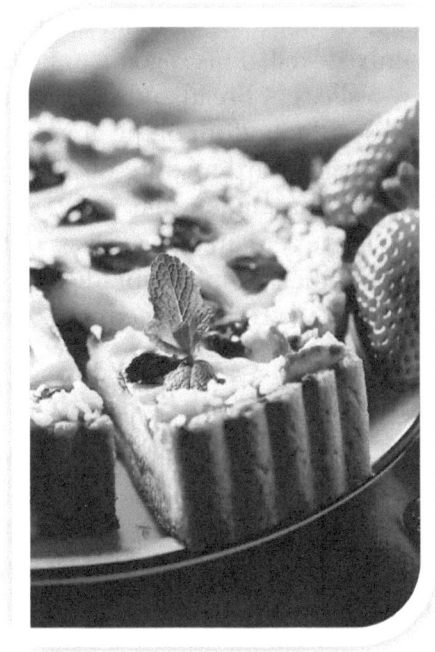

Prep Time: 15 minutes | **Cook Time:** 25 minutes | **Servings:** 4

Ingredients:

- 4 large eggs
- 1/2 cup milk
- 1/4 cup all-purpose flour
- 1/4 cup granulated sugar
- 1/2 teaspoon vanilla extract
- Pinch of salt
- 4 slices of bread (white or whole wheat)
- 1/4 cup fruit jam or preserves (e.g., raspberry, strawberry, or your favorite)
- 1 tablespoon unsalted butter
- Powdered sugar for dusting (optional)
- Fresh berries for garnish (optional)

Instructions:

1. **Preheat Oven:** Preheat your oven to 350°F (175°C). Grease a baking dish or an oven-safe skillet.
2. **Make Egg Mixture:** In a big bowl, mix eggs, milk, flour, sugar, vanilla, and a little bit of salt until everything is mixed well. This is going to be the creamy custard mixture.
3. **Assemble Layers:** Take two slices of bread and spread fruit jam evenly on each slice. Place the jam-covered slices at the bottom of the greased baking dish.
4. **Add Custard:** Pour half the egg custard mixture over the jam-covered bread slices. Let the bread sit in the custard for a little while.
5. **Top with More Bread:** Place the remaining two slices of bread on top of the first layer, creating a sandwich with the jam in the middle.
6. **Pour Remaining Custard:** Pour the remaining custard mixture evenly over the top layer of bread.
7. **Let It Rest:** Allow the torta to sit for 10-15 minutes | so the custard can fully soak into the bread.
8. **Bake:** Dot the top with small pieces of unsalted butter. Put the baking dish in the oven and cook for about 25 minutes | until the torta is firm and the top is golden brown.
9. **Cool Slightly:** Remove the torta from the oven and let it cool slightly.
10. **Dust with Powdered Sugar:** If desired, dust the top of the torta with powdered sugar for a sweet finish.
11. **Garnish and Serve:** Serve the Breakfast Torta with Jam warm. You can put fresh berries on top if you want.

Nutrition Information (per serving):

- Calories: 291 kcal
- Protein: 9g
- Carbohydrates: 42g
- Dietary Fiber: 2g
- Sugars: 22g
- Fat: 10g
- Saturated Fat: 4g
- Cholesterol: 175mg
- Sodium: 217mg
- Potassium: 137mg

CURRY-AVOCADO CRISPY EGG TOAST

Prep Time: 10 minutes | **Cook Time:** 10 minutes | **Servings:** 2

Ingredients:

- 2 large eggs
- 2 slices of whole-grain bread (or bread of your choice)
- 1 ripe avocado
- 1/2 teaspoon curry powder
- 1/4 teaspoon paprika
- Salt and black pepper to taste
- Olive oil for frying
- Fresh cilantro leaves for garnish (optional)
- Red pepper flakes for a hint of spice (optional)

Instructions:

1. **Toast Bread:** Begin by cooking the bread slices until they turn a golden brown color and become crunchy. Set them aside.
2. **Prepare Avocado Spread:** Cut the ready-to-eat avocado into two pieces, remove the big seed, and use a spoon to put the soft inside part into a bowl. Add the curry powder, paprika, a pinch of salt, and a dash of black pepper. Mix everything until you have a smooth and creamy avocado spread.

3. **Fry Eggs:** Heat olive oil in a non-stick skillet over medium heat. Break the eggs into the pan and cook them until they are cooked to how you like them. (e.g., sunny-side-up or over-easy).
4. **Assemble Toasts:** Spread the curry-spiced avocado mixture evenly over the toasted bread slices.
5. **Add Fried Eggs:** Carefully place a fried egg on each avocado-covered toast.
6. **Season:** Season the eggs with an additional pinch of salt and black pepper to taste.
7. **Garnish:** Garnish your Curry-Avocado Crispy Egg Toast with fresh cilantro leaves and a sprinkle of red pepper flakes for a touch of heat.
8. **Serve:** Serve your delicious toast immediately while it's still warm.

Nutrition Information (per serving, 1 toast):

- Calories: 318 kcal
- Protein: 12g
- Carbohydrates: 24g
- Dietary Fiber: 8g
- Sugars: 2g
- Fat: 21g
- Saturated Fat: 4g
- Cholesterol: 186mg
- Sodium: 247mg
- Potassium: 707mg

BUTTERNUT SQUASH & SPINACH TOAST

Prep Time: 15 minutes | **Cook Time:** 25 minutes | **Servings:** 2

Ingredients:

- 2 slices of whole-grain bread (or bread of your choice)
- 1 cup butternut squash cubes, peeled and roasted
- 1 cup fresh spinach leaves
- 1/4 cup goat cheese, crumbled
- 2 tablespoons olive oil
- 1 clove garlic, minced
- Salt and black pepper to taste
- Red pepper flakes for a hint of spice (optional)
- Fresh thyme leaves for garnish (optional)

Instructions:

1. **Preheat Oven:** Turn on your oven and set it to 400 degrees Fahrenheit or 200 degrees Celsius.
2. **Roast Butternut Squash:** Mix the butternut squash pieces with 1 tablespoon of olive oil, chopped garlic, salt, and black pepper. Put them on a baking sheet and cook in the oven for around 20-25 minutes | or until soft and slightly browned.

3. **Toast Bread:** While the butternut squash is roasting, toast the slices of bread until they are golden brown and crispy.
4. **Sauté Spinach:** Heat the rest of the olive oil in a pan on medium heat. Put the fresh spinach leaves in the pan and cook them for 2-3 minutes | until they shrink and soften. Put a little bit of salt and black pepper on it.
5. **Assemble Toasts:** Spread the crumbled goat cheese evenly over the toasted bread slices.
6. **Add Roasted Butternut Squash:** Place the roasted squash cubes on the goat cheese layer.
7. **Top with Sautéed Spinach:** Add the sautéed spinach to the butternut squash.
8. **Season and Garnish:** Add some red pepper flakes to the toast for a spicy taste. Then, put some fresh thyme leaves on top to make them smell nice.
9. **Serve:** Serve your Butternut Squash and spinach Toast immediately while it's still warm.

Nutrition Information (per serving, 1 toast):

- Calories: 261 kcal
- Protein: 8g
- Carbohydrates: 30g
- Dietary Fiber: 5g
- Sugars: 4g
- Fat: 14g
- Saturated Fat: 4g
- Cholesterol: 9mg
- Sodium: 284mg
- Potassium: 506mg

CHEESY AVOCADO OMELETTE

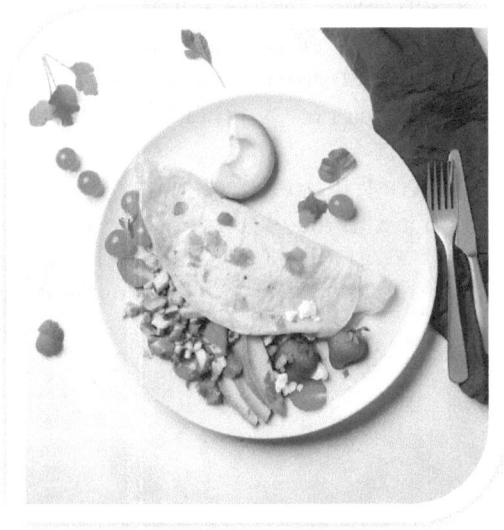

Prep Time: 10 minutes | **Cook Time:** 10 minutes | **Servings:** 1

Ingredients:

- 2 large eggs
- 1/2 ripe avocado, diced
- 1/4 cup shredded cheddar cheese
- 1/4 cup diced tomatoes
- 2 tablespoons diced red onion
- 1 tablespoon chopped fresh cilantro (optional)
- Salt and black pepper to taste
- 1 tablespoon olive oil or cooking spray for the skillet

Instructions:

1. **Prep Ingredients:** Dice the ripe avocado, tomatoes, and red onion. If using fresh cilantro, chop it finely.
2. **Whisk Eggs:** Beat the two big eggs in a bowl until the yellow and white parts are mixed. Add a small amount of salt and black pepper until it tastes good.
3. **Heat Skillet:** Heat a non-stick skillet over medium-high heat. Put olive oil or cooking spray in the skillet and cover the bottom.

4. **Pour Egg Mixture:** Pour the whisked egg mixture into the skillet. Allow it to cook for about 2-3 minutes | until the edges start to set.
5. **Add Avocado and Cheese:** Sprinkle the diced avocado evenly over one-half of the omelet. Follow with the shredded cheddar cheese.
6. **Fold Omelette:** Carefully fold the other half of the omelet over the avocado and cheese side, creating a half-moon shape.
7. **Cook Until Set:** Cook the omelet for another 2-3 minutes | or until the eggs are fully set and the cheese is melted.
8. **Add Toppings:** After you cook the omelet the way you want, take it out of the pan and put it on a plate. Top it with diced tomatoes, red onion, and chopped cilantro (if using).
9. **Serve:** Serve your Cheesy Avocado Omelette immediately while it's hot.

Nutrition Information (per serving):

- Calories: 418 kcal
- Protein: 20g
- Carbohydrates: 11g
- Dietary Fiber: 6g
- Sugars: 2g
- Fat: 34g
- Saturated Fat: 10g
- Cholesterol: 379mg
- Sodium: 371mg
- Potassium: 763mg

BREAKFAST CAKE WITH ROASTED GRAPE AND HAZELNUTS

Prep Time: 15 minutes | **Cook Time:** 35 minutes | **Servings:** 6

Ingredients:

- 1 cup all-purpose flour
- 1/2 cup whole wheat flour
- 1/2 cup granulated sugar
- 1/4 cup unsalted butter, softened
- 1/4 cup plain Greek yogurt
- 2 large eggs
- 1 teaspoon baking powder
- 1/2 teaspoon baking soda
- 1/2 teaspoon ground cinnamon
- Pinch of salt
- 1 cup red grapes, seedless
- 1/4 cup chopped hazelnuts
- 1 teaspoon vanilla extract
- Cooking spray or additional butter for greasing

Instructions:

1. **Preheat Oven:** Preheat your oven to 350°F (175°C). Use cooking spray or butter to coat a 9-inch round cake pan.

2. **Roast Grapes:** Place the red grapes on a baking sheet and roast them in the oven for 10-12 minutes. This will enhance their flavor and sweetness. Once roasted, set them aside to cool.
3. **Prepare Dry Ingredients:** In a bowl, blend the all-purpose flour, whole wheat flour, baking powder, baking soda, ground cinnamon, and a small amount of salt using a whisk. Set aside.
4. **Cream Butter and Sugar:** Mix the softened butter and sugar in a different bowl until it becomes light and fluffy.
5. **Add Eggs and Yogurt:** Put the eggs into the butter and sugar mixture. Mix it well after adding each egg. Combine the plain Greek yogurt and vanilla extract.
6. **Combine Wet and Dry Mixtures:** Gently combine the dry and wet ingredients until they are well mixed. Make sure you don't mix too much.
7. **Fold in Hazelnuts:** Gently fold the chopped hazelnuts into the cake batter.
8. **Add Roasted Grapes:** Carefully fold in the roasted grapes, ensuring they are evenly distributed in the batter.
9. **Transfer to Cake Pan:** Put the mixture into the cake pan that has been greased and spread it out so it is level.
10. **Bake:** Put the cake pan in the oven that has been warmed up beforehand and cook for around 25-30 minutes. Put a toothpick in the middle to determine if the cake is done. It is cooked if it comes out clean, and the cake looks brownish.
11. **Cool and Serve:** Let the breakfast cake cool in the pan for 10 minutes, then place it on a metal rack to let it cool down entirely.
12. **Slice and Enjoy:** Once cooled, slice the Breakfast Cake With Roasted Grape and hazelnuts into portions and serve.

Nutrition Information (per serving):

- Calories: 290 kcal
- Protein: 6g
- Carbohydrates: 44g
- Dietary Fiber: 3g
- Sugars: 21g
- Fat: 11g
- Saturated Fat: 5g
- Cholesterol: 72mg
- Sodium: 220mg
- Potassium: 181mg

TURKISH EGGS WITH GREEK YOGURT

Prep Time: 10 minutes | **Cook Time:** 10 minutes | **Servings:** 2

Ingredients:

- 4 large eggs
- 1 cup Greek yogurt
- 2 cloves garlic, minced
- 2 tablespoons unsalted butter
- 1 teaspoon olive oil
- 1/2 teaspoon ground cumin
- 1/2 teaspoon smoked paprika
- Salt and black pepper to taste
- Fresh cilantro leaves for garnish (optional)
- Red pepper flakes for a hint of spice (optional)
- Warm pita bread or crusty bread for serving

Instructions:

1. **Prepare Greek Yogurt:** Combine Greek yogurt and minced garlic in a bowl. Mix well and set aside.
2. **Poach Eggs:** Put some water in a pot and heat it gently on the stove. Put a little bit of vinegar into the boiling water. Crack each egg into a small bowl and gently slide them

into the simmering water. Poach the eggs for 3-4 minutes | until the egg whites are set, but the yolks are still runny. Use a spoon with holes to remove the poached eggs cautiously and put them on a plate covered with paper towels to remove extra water.

3. **Prepare Spiced Butter:** In a little pan, heat the butter and olive oil on medium heat until the butter is all melted. Mix in the cumin and smoked paprika powder. Cook the food for about 1-2 minutes | until it smells nice. Add salt and black pepper to your food until it tastes good.

4. **Assemble Dish:** To serve, evenly spread the garlic-infused Greek yogurt on two plates. Place the poached eggs on top of the yogurt.

5. **Drizzle Spiced Butter:** Drizzle the spiced butter mixture over the poached eggs and yogurt.

6. **Garnish:** Sprinkle some fresh cilantro leaves on top for taste and appearance. You can add red pepper flakes for a spicy flavor if you want to.

7. **Serve:** Serve your Turkish Eggs with Greek Yogurt with warm pita bread or crusty bread on the side for dipping.

Nutrition Information (per serving):

- Calories: 364 kcal
- Protein: 23g
- Carbohydrates: 8g
- Dietary Fiber: 1g
- Sugars: 4g
- Fat: 28g
- Saturated Fat: 13g
- Cholesterol: 412mg
- Sodium: 105mg
- Potassium: 360mg

SWEET GREEK AVOCADO TOAST

Prep Time: 10 minutes | **Cook Time:** 5 minutes | **Servings:** 2

Ingredients:

- 2 slices of whole-grain bread (or bread of your choice)
- 1 ripe avocado
- 1/2 cup Greek yogurt
- 2 tablespoons honey
- 1/4 teaspoon ground cinnamon
- 1/4 cup fresh berries (e.g., strawberries, blueberries, or raspberries)
- 2 tablespoons chopped nuts (e.g., almonds or walnuts), toasted
- Fresh mint leaves for garnish (optional)

Instructions:

1. **Toast Bread:** Begin by cooking the pieces of bread until they turn a nice, golden brown color and become crunchy. Put them away.
2. **Prepare Avocado Spread:** Cut the ripe avocado into two pieces, take out the big seed inside, and use a spoon to put the inside of the avocado into a bowl. Make the avocado into a smooth texture by crushing or blending it.
3. **Sweeten Greek Yogurt:** In a separate bowl, combine the Greek yogurt, honey, and ground cinnamon. Mix well to sweeten the yogurt.
4. **Assemble Toasts:** Spread the mashed avocado evenly over the toasted bread slices.
5. **Add Sweetened Greek Yogurt:** Dollop the sweetened Greek yogurt on top of the avocado layer.

41

6. **Top with Berries:** Scatter fresh berries over the yogurt layer. You can use a single type of berry or a mix of your favorites.
7. **Sprinkle with Toasted Nuts:** Sprinkle the chopped and toasted nuts over the berries for added crunch and flavor.
8. **Garnish:** If desired, garnish your Sweet Greek Avocado Toast with fresh mint leaves for a refreshing touch.
9. **Serve:** Serve your delicious Sweet Greek Avocado Toast immediately while it's still fresh and vibrant.

Nutrition Information (per serving, 1 toast):

- Calories: 289 kcal
- Protein: 7g
- Carbohydrates: 30g
- Dietary Fiber: 7g
- Sugars: 14g
- Fat: 18g
- Saturated Fat: 3g
- Cholesterol: 3mg
- Sodium: 170mg
- Potassium: 497mg

SHAKSHUKA

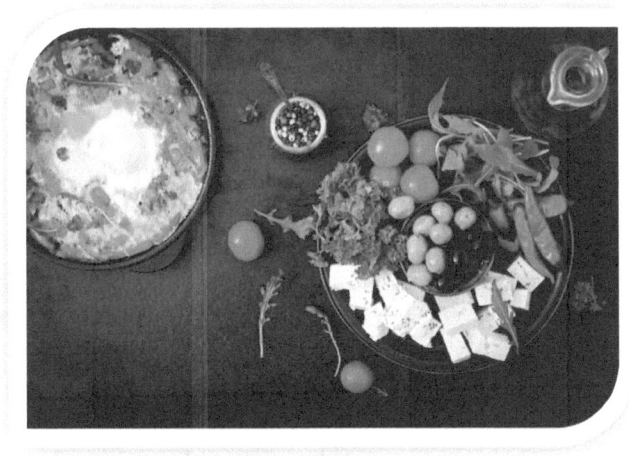

Prep Time: 10 minutes | **Cook Time:** 25 minutes | **Servings:** 2-3

Ingredients:

- 2 tablespoons olive oil
- 1 onion, finely chopped
- 1 red bell pepper, diced
- 2 cloves garlic, minced
- 1 teaspoon ground cumin
- 1 teaspoon ground paprika
- 1/2 teaspoon ground cayenne pepper (adjust to taste)
- 1 can (14 ounces) diced tomatoes
- Salt and black pepper to taste
- 4-6 large eggs
- Fresh parsley or cilantro leaves for garnish
- Feta cheese or crumbled goat cheese for topping (optional)
- Crusty bread or pita for serving

Instructions:

1. **Sauté Vegetables:** Heat the olive oil in a large, deep skillet or pan over medium heat. Add the chopped onion and diced red bell pepper. Sauté for about 5 minutes | until the vegetables soften and the onion becomes translucent.
2. **Add Garlic and Spices:** Add the minced garlic, ground cumin, ground paprika, and ground cayenne pepper (adjust to your preferred level of spiciness). Cook for an additional 1-2 minutes | until fragrant.
3. **Add Tomatoes:** Pour in the can of diced tomatoes with their juice. Season with salt and black pepper to taste. Stir well to combine all the ingredients. Allow the mixture to simmer for 10-15 minutes | until it thickens slightly.
4. **Make Indentations for Eggs:** Using a spoon, create small indentations or "wells" in the tomato mixture for the eggs. Crack each egg and gently slide it into one of the indentations.
5. **Simmer Eggs:** Cover the skillet and let the eggs cook in the tomato mixture for 5-7 minutes, or until the egg whites are set, but the yolks are still slightly runny. You can adjust the cooking time to achieve your preferred level of yolk doneness.
6. **Garnish and Serve:** Once the eggs are cooked to your liking, garnish the Shakshuka with fresh parsley or cilantro leaves. Optionally, you can crumble feta cheese or goat cheese over the top. Serve the Shakshuka directly from the skillet with crusty bread or pita for dipping.

Nutrition Information (per serving, based on 3 servings):

- Calories: 225 kcal
- Protein: 10g
- Carbohydrates: 15g
- Dietary Fiber: 4g
- Sugars: 7g
- Fat: 15g
- Saturated Fat: 3g
- Cholesterol: 186mg
- Sodium: 546mg
- Potassium: 640mg

CHAPTER 3:
WHOLESOME
LUNCHES

PESTO CHICKEN QUINOA BOWLS

Prep Time: 15 minutes | **Cook Time:** 20 minutes | **Servings:** 2

Ingredients:

For the Pesto Chicken:

- 2 boneless, skinless chicken breasts
- 2 tablespoons olive oil
- Salt and black pepper to taste
- 2 tablespoons pesto sauce (store-bought or homemade)

For the Quinoa Bowl:

- 1 cup quinoa, rinsed and drained
- 2 cups water or chicken broth (for cooking quinoa)
- 1 cup cherry tomatoes, halved
- 1 cup fresh spinach leaves
- 1/2 cup roasted red bell peppers, sliced
- 1/4 cup Kalamata olives, pitted and sliced

- 1/4 cup crumbled feta cheese (optional)
- Lemon wedges for serving

Instructions:

For the Pesto Chicken:

1. **Preheat Oven:** Preheat your oven to 375°F (190°C).
2. **Season Chicken:** Season the chicken breasts with salt and black pepper to taste.
3. **Sear Chicken:** Warm the olive oil over medium-high warm in an ovenproof skillet. Burn the chicken breasts for 2-3 minutes | per side until brilliant brown.
4. **Spread Pesto:** Remove the skillet from the heat, and spread a tablespoon of pesto sauce over each chicken breast.
5. **Bake:** Place the skillet in the preheated oven and bake for 15-20 minutes | until the chicken is cooked and no longer pink in the center. The internal temperature should reach 165°F (74°C).
6. **Slice and Set Aside:** Remove the chicken from the oven and let it rest for a few minutes. Then, slice it into thin strips.

For the Quinoa Bowl:

1. **Cook Quinoa:** Combine the rinsed quinoa and water (or chicken broth) in a medium saucepan. Heat the mixture until it starts bubbling, then lower the heat, put a lid on, and let it cook gently for around 15 minutes | until the quinoa is fully cooked and the liquid has been soaked up. Remove from heat and fluff with a fork.
2. **Assemble Bowls:** Divide the cooked quinoa between two bowls. Top with sliced cherry tomatoes, fresh spinach leaves, roasted red bell peppers, and Kalamata olives.
3. **Add Pesto Chicken:** Arrange the sliced pesto chicken over the quinoa and vegetable mixture.
4. **Optional Toppings:** If desired, sprinkle crumbled feta cheese over the bowls for extra flavor.
5. **Serve:** Serve the Pesto Chicken Quinoa Bowls with lemon wedges on the side for a refreshing touch. Squeeze lemon juice over the bowls before enjoying.

Nutrition Information (per serving):

- Calories: 570 kcal
- Protein: 39g
- Carbohydrates: 51g
- Dietary Fiber: 6g
- Sugars: 4g
- Fat: 24g

- Saturated Fat: 5g
- Cholesterol: 100mg
- Sodium: 780mg
- Potassium: 990mg

SALMON RICE BOWL

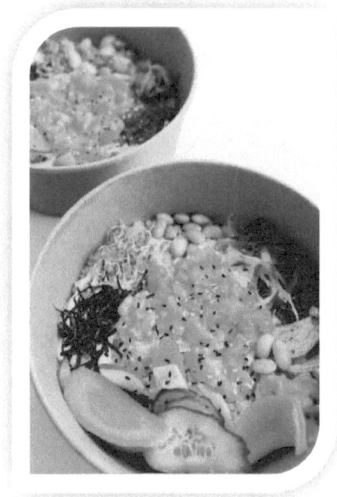

Prep Time: 15 minutes | **Cook Time:** 20 minutes | **Servings:** 2

Ingredients:

For the Salmon:

- 2 salmon fillets (about 6 ounces each)
- 1 tablespoon olive oil
- Salt and black pepper to taste
- 1 teaspoon lemon zest
- 1 tablespoon lemon juice
- 1 clove garlic, minced
- 1/2 teaspoon dried oregano

For the Rice Bowl:

- 1 cup cooked brown rice
- 1 cup cucumber, diced
- 1 cup cherry tomatoes, halved
- 1/2 cup red onion, thinly sliced
- 1/4 cup Kalamata olives, pitted and sliced
- 1/4 cup crumbled feta cheese

- Fresh dill or parsley for garnish
- Lemon wedges for serving

Instructions:

For the Salmon:

1. **Marinate Salmon:** In a small bowl, combine the olive oil, salt, black pepper, lemon zest, lemon juice, minced garlic, and dried oregano. Mix well to create the marinade.
2. **Marinate Salmon:** Put the pieces of salmon in a flat dish and pour the sauce on top of them. Ensure the salmon is coated evenly. Let it marinate for about 10 minutes | while you prepare the other ingredients.
3. **Cook Salmon:** Heat a skillet or pan over medium-high heat. Put a small amount of olive oil to stop things from sticking. Put the salmon pieces in the frying pan with the skin facing down and cook for 3-4 minutes | on each side. Check if the salmon is cooked by seeing if it breaks apart easily with a fork and has a nice crust. Remove from heat.

For the Rice Bowl:

1. **Assemble Bowls:** Divide the cooked brown rice between two bowls. Arrange the diced cucumber, halved cherry tomatoes, thinly sliced red onion, and sliced Kalamata olives over the rice.
2. **Add Salmon:** Place one cooked salmon fillet in each rice bowl.
3. **Sprinkle Feta Cheese:** Sprinkle crumbled feta cheese evenly over the bowls.
4. **Garnish:** Garnish with fresh dill or parsley for flavor and a burst of color.
5. **Serve:** Serve the Salmon Rice Bowls with lemon wedges on the side. Squeeze lemon juice over the bowls before enjoying.

Nutrition Information (per serving):

- Calories: 487 kcal
- Protein: 32g
- Carbohydrates: 36g
- Dietary Fiber: 5g
- Sugars: 5g
- Fat: 23g
- Saturated Fat: 6g
- Cholesterol: 85mg
- Sodium: 560mg
- Potassium: 959mg

TOMATO & AVOCADO CHEESE SANDWICH

Prep Time: 10 minutes | **Cook Time:** 0 minutes | **Servings:** 2

Ingredients:

- 4 slices of whole-grain bread
- 1 large ripe avocado, sliced
- 1 large tomato, sliced
- 4 slices of your favorite cheese (e.g., cheddar, Swiss, or provolone)
- 2 tablespoons hummus (store-bought or homemade)
- Fresh basil leaves for garnish (optional)
- Salt and black pepper to taste

Instructions:

1. **Assemble the Sandwiches:** Lay out the four slices of whole-grain bread. On two of the slices, spread a tablespoon of hummus on each.
2. **Add Cheese:** Put a piece of cheese on the bread with hummus for each sandwich.
3. **Layer Avocado and Tomato:** Arrange the sliced avocado on top of the cheese, followed by the sliced tomato.
4. **Season:** Add flavor to the avocado and tomato with a pinch of salt and a sprinkle of black pepper.

5. **Top with Basil (Optional):** Add fresh basil leaves to the tomato slices for freshness and aroma if desired.
6. **Top with Second Slice:** Place the remaining slices of bread on top to complete the sandwiches.
7. **Cut and Serve:** Diagonally cut each sandwich in half to create two triangular halves. Serve immediately.

Nutrition Information (per serving, 1 sandwich):

- Calories: 394 kcal
- Protein: 13g
- Carbohydrates: 33g
- Dietary Fiber: 11g
- Sugars: 4g
- Fat: 25g
- Saturated Fat: 9g
- Cholesterol: 30mg
- Sodium: 487mg
- Potassium: 712mg

SALMON-STUFFED AVOCADOS

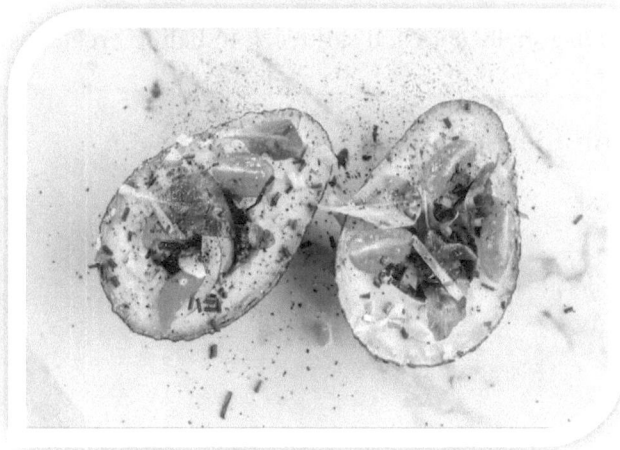

Prep Time: 15 minutes | **Cook Time:** 0 minutes | **Servings:** 2

Ingredients:

- 2 ripe avocados, halved and pitted
- 1 can (6 ounces) of canned salmon, drained
- 2 tablespoons Greek yogurt
- 1/4 cup cucumber, finely diced
- 1/4 cup of red bell pepper that has been cut into small pieces.
- 2 tablespoons red onion, finely diced
- 2 tablespoons fresh dill, chopped
- 1 tablespoon lemon juice
- Salt and black pepper to taste
- Fresh dill sprigs for garnish (optional)

Instructions:

1. **Prepare the Avocados:** Cut the ripe avocados in half lengthwise and remove the pits. Carefully scoop a bit of the flesh from each avocado half to create a larger cavity for the stuffing. Save the scooped-out avocado for another use, or chop it and add it to the filling.

2. **Prepare the Filling:** Mix the canned salmon in a bowl, Greek yogurt, finely diced cucumber, red bell pepper, red onion, chopped fresh dill, and lemon juice. Mix well to combine all the ingredients. Sprinkle some salt and black pepper as per your liking.
3. **Stuff the Avocado Halves:** Spoon the salmon mixture into the hollowed-out halves, dividing it evenly among them. Press down gently to pack the filling.
4. **Garnish:** Garnish each stuffed avocado half with a sprig of fresh dill for presentation.
5. **Serve:** Serve the Salmon-Stuffed Avocados immediately, and enjoy this flavorful and nutritious dish!

Nutrition Information (per serving, 1 stuffed avocado half):

- Calories: 274 kcal
- Protein: 18g
- Carbohydrates: 12g
- Dietary Fiber: 8g
- Sugars: 2g
- Fat: 18g
- Saturated Fat: 3g
- Cholesterol: 29mg
- Sodium: 421mg
- Potassium: 875mg

CUCUMBER-CHICKEN GREEN GODDESS WRAP

Prep Time: 15 minutes | **Cook Time:** 10 minutes | (for chicken, if not using pre-cooked) **Servings:** 2 wraps

Ingredients:

For the Green Goddess Dressing:

- 1/2 cup Greek yogurt
- 2 tablespoons fresh parsley, chopped
- 2 tablespoons fresh basil, chopped
- 1 tablespoon fresh chives, chopped
- 1 clove garlic, minced
- 1 tablespoon lemon juice
- Salt and black pepper to taste

For the Wrap:

- 2 whole-grain tortillas or wraps
- 1 cup cooked chicken breast, shredded (you can also use rotisserie chicken)
- 1 cup cucumber, thinly sliced

- 1 cup mixed greens or lettuce leaves
- 1/2 cup cherry tomatoes, halved
- 1/4 cup red onion, thinly sliced
- 1/4 cup feta cheese, crumbled (optional)
- Fresh basil leaves for garnish (optional)

Instructions:

For the Green Goddess Dressing:

1. Mix Greek yogurt, parsley, basil, chives, garlic, lemon juice, salt, and black pepper in a blender or food processor.
2. Blend until the ingredients are well combined, and the dressing is smooth. Taste and adjust the seasoning if needed. Set aside.

For the Wrap:

1. If using uncooked chicken breast, season it with salt and pepper and cook it in a skillet over medium-high heat with olive oil until it's cooked through (about 4-5 minutes | per side). Allow it to cool slightly before shredding.
2. Lay out the whole-grain tortillas or wraps on a clean surface.
3. Spread a generous spoonful of the prepared Green Goddess Dressing onto each tortilla, leaving about an inch from the edges.
4. Divide the shredded chicken evenly between the two tortillas, placing it on top of the dressing.
5. Add the thinly sliced cucumber, mixed greens, cherry tomatoes, and thinly sliced red onion to the chicken.
6. If desired, sprinkle crumbled feta cheese evenly over the fillings.
7. Use fresh basil leaves to make the dish tastier and more visually appealing.
8. Carefully fold in the sides of each tortilla and then roll it up from the bottom to create a wrap.
9. Slice the wraps in half diagonally and serve immediately.

Nutrition Information (per serving, 1 wrap):

- Calories: 425 kcal
- Protein: 32g
- Carbohydrates: 30g
- Dietary Fiber: 5g
- Sugars: 6g
- Fat: 19g

- Saturated Fat: 5g
- Cholesterol: 75mg
- Sodium: 554mg
- Potassium: 590mg

CRISPY SMOKED TOFU AND COLESLAW WRAPS

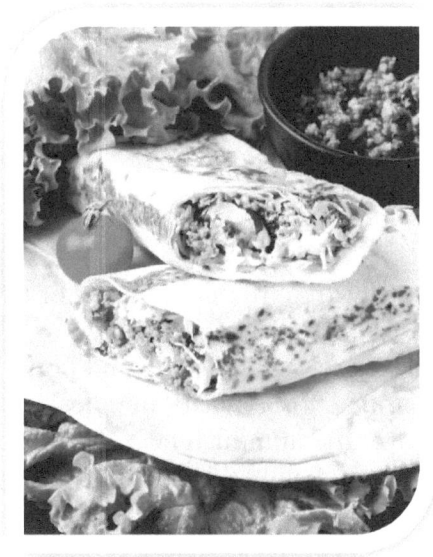

Prep Time: 20 minutes | **Cook Time:** 20 minutes | **Servings:** 2 wraps

Ingredients:

For the Smoked Tofu:

- 8 ounces (about 1/2 block) smoked tofu, sliced into strips
- 1 tablespoon olive oil
- 1 tablespoon soy sauce or tamari
- 1/2 teaspoon smoked paprika
- 1/2 teaspoon garlic powder
- 1/4 teaspoon black pepper

For the Coleslaw:

- 1 1/2 cups shredded cabbage (green or purple)
- 1/2 cup grated carrots
- 1/4 cup Greek yogurt
- 1 tablespoon mayonnaise
- 1 tablespoon apple cider vinegar

- 1 teaspoon honey or maple syrup
- Salt and black pepper to taste

For the Wraps:

- 2 whole-grain or whole-wheat tortillas
- Fresh cilantro leaves for garnish (optional)

Instructions:

For the Smoked Tofu:

1. Mix a small marinade bowl with olive oil, soy sauce or tamari, smoked paprika, garlic powder, and black pepper.
2. Place the sliced smoked tofu in a shallow dish and pour the marinade. Toss to coat the tofu evenly. Let it marinate for about 10 minutes.
3. Heat a non-stick skillet over medium-high heat. Add the marinated tofu strips and cook for 3-4 minutes | per side until they become crispy and browned. Remove from heat.

For the Coleslaw:

1. In a bowl, mix the sliced cabbage and shredded carrots.
2. Mix the Greek yogurt, mayonnaise, apple cider vinegar, honey, salt, and black pepper in a small bowl to make the coleslaw dressing.
3. Pour the dressing over the cabbage and carrots. Toss to coat the vegetables evenly.

For the Wraps:

1. Lay out the whole-grain or whole-wheat tortillas on a clean surface.
2. Split the coleslaw mixture into two equal parts. Put each part onto a tortilla and spread it in the middle.
3. Arrange the crispy smoked tofu strips on top of the coleslaw.
4. Put fresh cilantro leaves on top for extra taste and a burst of color.
5. Carefully fold in the sides of each tortilla and then roll it up from the bottom to create a wrap.
6. Slice the wraps in half diagonally and serve immediately.

Nutrition Information (per serving, 1 wrap):

- Calories: 390 kcal
- Protein: 19g
- Carbohydrates: 37g

- Dietary Fiber: 5g
- Sugars: 7g
- Fat: 19g
- Saturated Fat: 3g
- Cholesterol: 4mg
- Sodium: 777mg
- Potassium: 449mg

EGG SANDWICHES WITH ROSEMARY, TOMATO & FETA

Prep Time: 10 minutes | **Cook Time:** 10 minutes | **Servings:** 2 sandwiches

Ingredients:

- 4 large eggs
- 2 tablespoons milk
- Salt and black pepper to taste
- 1 tablespoon fresh rosemary, chopped
- 2 tablespoons olive oil
- 4 slices of whole-grain or whole-wheat bread
- 1 large tomato, sliced
- 1/2 cup crumbled feta cheese
- Fresh basil leaves for garnish (optional)

Instructions:

1. **Scramble the Eggs:** In a bowl, mix the big eggs, milk, salt, and black pepper with a whisk. Mix in the diced rosemary.
2. **Cook the Eggs:** Heat olive oil in a non-stick skillet over medium-high heat. Put the egg mixture into the frying pan and stir gently until the eggs are softly cooked and a little creamy. Take it off the heat source.
3. **Toast the Bread:** Toast the whole-grain or whole-wheat bread slices until they're crispy and golden.
4. **Assemble the Sandwiches:** Lay out two slices of toasted bread. Divide the scrambled eggs evenly between the two slices, spreading them out.
5. **Add Tomato Slices:** Place tomato slices on top of the eggs.
6. **Sprinkle with Feta:** Sprinkle crumbled feta cheese evenly over the tomatoes.
7. **Garnish (Optional):** Garnish with fresh basil leaves for added flavor and a pop of color.
8. **Top with remaining Bread:** Place the two slices of toasted bread on top to complete the sandwiches.
9. **Slice and Serve:** Cut each sandwich in half diagonally and serve immediately.

Nutrition Information (per serving, 1 sandwich):

- Calories: 347 kcal
- Protein: 16g
- Carbohydrates: 20g
- Dietary Fiber: 4g
- Sugars: 3g
- Fat: 23g
- Saturated Fat: 8g
- Cholesterol: 363mg
- Sodium: 667mg
- Potassium: 410mg

CITRUS LIME TOFU SALAD

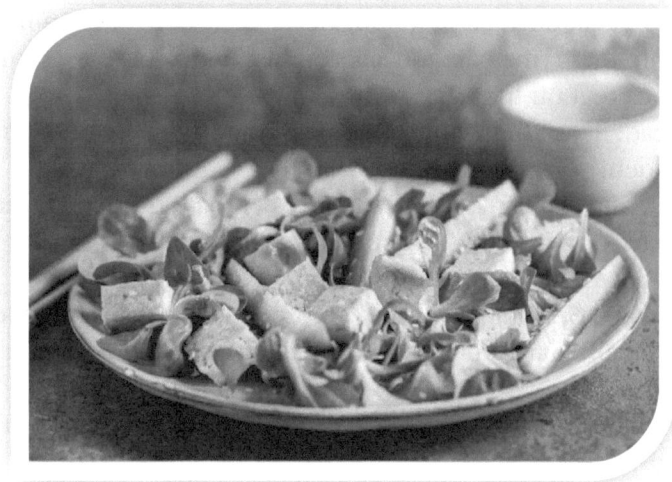

Prep Time: 15 minutes | **Cook Time:** 10 minutes | **Servings:** 2

Ingredients:

For the Tofu:

- 8 ounces extra-firm tofu, cubed
- 1 tablespoon olive oil
- 1 tablespoon soy sauce or tamari
- 1/2 teaspoon ground cumin
- 1/2 teaspoon paprika
- Salt and black pepper to taste

For the Salad:

- 4 cups mixed salad greens (e.g., lettuce, spinach, arugula)
- 1 cup cherry tomatoes, halved
- 1/2 cucumber, sliced
- 1/4 red onion, thinly sliced
- 1/4 cup fresh cilantro leaves, chopped
- 1/4 cup fresh mint leaves, chopped

For the Citrus-Lime Dressing:

- 2 tablespoons fresh lime juice
- 1 tablespoon olive oil
- 1 teaspoon honey or maple syrup (optional for sweetness)
- Salt and black pepper to taste
- Zest of 1 lime for garnish (optional)

Instructions:

For the Tofu:

1. **Press Tofu:** Start by pressing the tofu to remove excess moisture. Put a towel or paper on top of the tofu and put something heavy on it (e.g., a cast-iron skillet or a can of beans) on top. Press for about 10-15 minutes.
2. **Marinate Tofu:** In a bowl, whisk together the olive oil, soy sauce or tamari, ground cumin, paprika, salt, and black pepper. Chop the firm tofu into square pieces and mix them in the flavored liquid. Let it marinate for about 10 minutes.
3. **Cook Tofu:** Heat a skillet or pan over medium-high heat. Add a small amount of olive oil to prevent things from getting stuck. Place the marinated tofu cubes in the skillet and cook for 2-3 minutes | per side or until golden and crispy. Remove from heat.

For the Salad:

1. **Prepare Salad Greens:** Divide the mixed salad greens between two serving plates.
2. **Add Veggies:** Arrange the cherry tomato halves, sliced cucumber, thinly sliced red onion, chopped fresh cilantro, and chopped fresh mint over the salad greens.

For the Citrus-Lime Dressing:

1. **Prepare Dressing:** In a small bowl, whisk together the fresh lime juice, olive oil, honey, salt, and black pepper to create the dressing.

Assemble the Salad:

2. **Top with Tofu:** Place the crispy marinated tofu cubes on top of the salad.
3. **Drizzle with Dressing:** Drizzle the citrus lime dressing over the salad and tofu.
4. **Garnish (Optional):** Garnish with lime zest for added flavor and freshness.
5. **Serve:** Serve the Citrus Lime Tofu Salad immediately as a refreshing and vibrant Mediterranean-inspired dish.

Nutrition Information (per serving):

- Calories: 318 kcal
- Protein: 14g
- Carbohydrates: 23g
- Dietary Fiber: 6g
- Sugars: 10g
- Fat: 22g
- Saturated Fat: 3g
- Cholesterol: 0mg
- Sodium: 345mg
- Potassium: 831mg

STUFFED SWEET POTATO WITH HUMMUS DRESSING

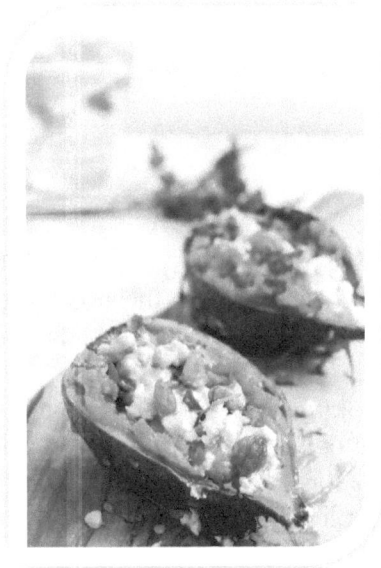

Prep Time: 10 minutes | **Cook Time:** 45 minutes | **Servings:** 2

Ingredients:

For the Stuffed Sweet Potatoes:

- 2 medium sweet potatoes
- 1 can (15 ounces) chickpeas, drained and rinsed
- 1 tablespoon olive oil
- 1 teaspoon ground cumin
- 1/2 teaspoon smoked paprika
- Salt and black pepper to taste
- 1/2 cup cherry tomatoes, halved
- 1/4 cup red onion, finely chopped
- 2 tablespoons fresh cilantro or parsley, chopped
- 2 tablespoons crumbled feta cheese (optional)
- Lemon wedges for garnish (optional)

For the Hummus Dressing:

- 1/4 cup hummus (store-bought or homemade)
- 1 tablespoon fresh lemon juice
- 1 tablespoon olive oil
- 1 clove garlic, minced
- Salt and black pepper to taste

Instructions:

For the Stuffed Sweet Potatoes:

1. **Preheat the oven** to 400°F (200°C).
2. **Prepare Sweet Potatoes:** Wash and scrub the sweet potatoes thoroughly. Poke holes in each sweet potato with a fork. Place them on a baking sheet lined with parchment paper.
3. **Roast Sweet Potatoes:** Cook the sweet potatoes on the stove for almost 40-45 minutes | or until they are delicate when punctured with a fork.
4. **Prepare Chickpeas:** While the sweet potatoes are roasting, in a bowl, toss the drained and rinsed chickpeas with olive oil, ground cumin, smoked paprika, salt, and black pepper.
5. **Roast Chickpeas:** Spread the seasoned chickpeas on a separate baking sheet and roast in the same oven for about 15-20 minutes | or until crispy.
6. **Assemble Stuffed Sweet Potatoes:** Let them cool slightly once the sweet potatoes are done. Cut each sweet potato in half lengthwise, careful not to cut all the way through. Fluff the flesh with a fork.
7. **Add Toppings:** Top each sweet potato half with the roasted chickpeas, halved cherry tomatoes, finely chopped red onion, fresh cilantro or parsley, and crumbled feta cheese (if using).

For the Hummus Dressing:

1. **Prepare Dressing:** In a bowl, whisk together the hummus, fresh lemon juice, olive oil, minced garlic, black pepper, and salt to create the dressing.

To Serve:

1. **Drizzle with Dressing:** Drizzle the hummus dressing generously over the stuffed sweet potatoes.
2. **Garnish (Optional):** Garnish with lemon wedges for added zest and freshness.
3. **Serve:** Serve the Stuffed Sweet Potato with Hummus Dressing as a nutritious and flavorful Mediterranean-inspired dish.

Nutrition Information (per serving, 1 stuffed sweet potato half):

- Calories: 352 kcal
- Protein: 11g
- Carbohydrates: 54g
- Dietary Fiber: 12g
- Sugars: 10g
- Fat: 11g
- Saturated Fat: 2g
- Cholesterol: 4mg
- Sodium: 603mg
- Potassium: 1040mg

WEST COAST AVOCADO TOAST

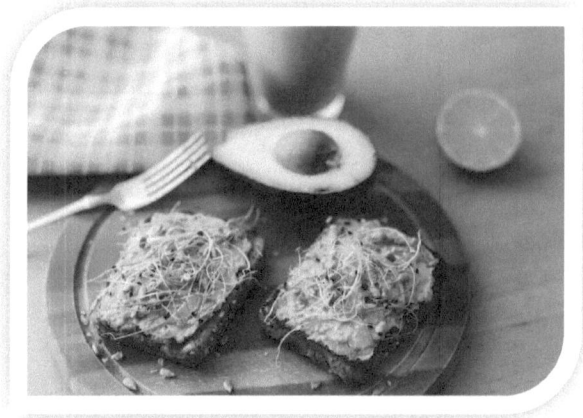

Prep Time: 10 minutes | **Cook Time:** 5 minutes | **Servings:** 2

Ingredients:

- 2 slices of whole-grain or artisanal bread
- 1 large ripe avocado
- 1 small lemon, juiced
- Use half a teaspoon of red pepper flakes (change the amount if you prefer less or more spice).
- Salt and black pepper to taste
- 1/4 cup cherry tomatoes, halved
- 1/4 cup cucumber, thinly sliced
- 1/4 cup radishes, thinly sliced
- 1/4 cup red onion, thinly sliced
- w1/4 cup fresh cilantro or parsley, chopped
- 2 poached or fried eggs (optional)
- Toasted sesame seeds for garnish (optional)

Instructions:

1. **Toast the Bread:** Toast the n or artisanal bread slices untslices
2. **Prepare the Avocado:** Cut the ripe avocado in half and remove the pit. Put the avocado in a bowl and crush it with a fork.

3. **Season the Avocado:** Put the juice from a fresh lemon, red pepper flakes, salt, and black pepper into the mashed avocado. Mix well to combine.
4. **Assemble the Avocado Toast:** Spread the seasoned mashed avocado evenly over the toasted bread slices.
5. **Add Fresh Veggies:** Layer the halved cherry tomatoes, thinly sliced cucumber, radishes, and red onion on top of the avocado.
6. **Garnish:** Sprinkle fresh cilantro or parsley over the veggies. Add poached or fried eggs to each toast for extra protein if desired.
7. **Additional Garnish (Optional):** To finish, sprinkle toasted sesame seeds over the avocado toast for added texture and flavor.
8. **Serve:** Serve the West Coast Avocado Toast immediately as a vibrant and satisfying Mediterranean-inspired breakfast or brunch.

Nutrition Information (per serving, 1 slice of toast):

- Calories: 247 kcal
- Protein: 7g
- Carbohydrates: 26g
- Dietary Fiber: 8g
- Sugars: 3g
- Fat: 15g
- Saturated Fat: 2g
- Cholesterol: 0mg
- Sodium: 208mg
- Potassium: 748mg

CHAPTER 4: DELICIOUS DINNERS

SHRIMP AND VEGETABLE SKEWERS

Prep Time: 20 minutes | **Cook Time:** 10 minutes | **Servings:** 2

Ingredients:

For the Marinade:

- 2 tablespoons olive oil
- 2 tablespoons fresh lemon juice
- 2 cloves garlic, minced
- 1 teaspoon dried oregano
- Salt and black pepper to taste

For the Skewers:

- 12 large shrimp, peeled and deveined
- 1 red bell pepper, cut into chunks
- 1 yellow bell pepper, cut into chunks
- 1 red onion, cut into chunks
- 1 zucchini, sliced into rounds
- 1 lemon, sliced into rounds
- Soak wooden sticks in water for half an hour.

Instructions:

<u>For the Marinade:</u>

1. Mix the marinade in a bowl with olive oil, lemon juice, garlic, oregano, salt, and pepper.

<u>For the Skewers:</u>

1. **Preheat the Grill:** Preheat your grill to medium-high heat.
2. **Assemble the Skewers:** Thread the shrimp, red bell pepper chunks, yellow bell pepper chunks, red onion chunks, zucchini rounds, and lemon rounds alternately onto the soaked wooden skewers.
3. **Brush with Marinade:** Brush the marinade generously over the skewers, coating them evenly.
4. **Grill the Skewers:** Put the skewers on the heated grill and cook for approximately 3-4 minutes | on each side until the shrimp turn pink and opaque and the vegetables are tender and slightly charred.
5. **Baste with Marinade:** Baste the skewers with additional marinade for extra flavor while grilling.
6. **Serve:** Serve the Shrimp and Vegetable Skewers immediately as a delicious and healthy Mediterranean-inspired dish.

Nutrition Information (per serving, 6 skewers):

- Calories: 226 kcal
- Protein: 17g
- Carbohydrates: 20g
- Dietary Fiber: 5g
- Sugars: 8g
- Fat: 9g
- Saturated Fat: 1g
- Cholesterol: 95mg
- Sodium: 129mg
- Potassium: 732mg

SALMON WITH PESTO AND BLISTERED TOMATOES

Prep Time: 15 minutes | **Cook Time:** 15 minutes | **Servings:** 2

Ingredients:

For the Pesto:

- 2 cups fresh basil leaves, packed
- 1/2 cup grated Parmesan cheese
- 1/4 cup pine nuts
- 2 cloves garlic, minced
- 1/2 cup extra-virgin olive oil
- Salt and black pepper to taste

For the Salmon:

- 2 salmon fillets (6-8 ounces each)
- Salt and black pepper to taste
- 2 tablespoons olive oil
- 1 pint cherry tomatoes
- 2 tablespoons balsamic vinegar
- Fresh basil leaves for garnish (optional)

Instructions:

For the Pesto:

1. **Prepare the Pesto:** In a food processor, combine the fresh basil leaves, grated Parmesan cheese, pine nuts, and minced garlic. Pulse until the ingredients are finely chopped.
2. **Add Olive Oil:** While the food processor is on, slowly pour the extra-virgin olive oil until the pesto becomes smooth and creamy. Sprinkle some salt and black pepper as much as you like. Leave or move something to the side or out of the way.

For the Salmon:

1. **Turn on your oven and set the temperature to 375°F (190°C).**
2. **Season the Salmon:** Season the salmon fillets with salt and black pepper to taste.
3. **Sear the Salmon:** Heat olive oil over medium-high heat in an oven-safe skillet. When the pan is hot, put the salmon fillets in with the skin facing down. Sear for about 2-3 minutes | until the skin is crispy.
4. **Flip and Add Tomatoes:** Turn over the salmon pieces and put the cherry tomatoes into the frying pan. Drizzle the balsamic vinegar over the tomatoes.
5. **Roast in the Oven:** Put the skillet in the oven you have already heated. Cook the salmon for around 10-12 minutes | or until it is done and breaks apart easily when you poke it with a fork.
6. **Serve:** Serve the salmon fillets with a generous dollop of pesto on top and the blistered tomatoes on the side. Garnish with fresh basil leaves if desired.

Nutrition Information (per serving, 1 salmon fillet with pesto and tomatoes):

- Calories: 580 kcal
- Protein: 37g
- Carbohydrates: 9g
- Dietary Fiber: 2g
- Sugars: 4g
- Fat: 45g
- Saturated Fat: 8g
- Cholesterol: 92mg
- Sodium: 420mg
- Potassium: 1010mg

FALL ROASTED VEGETABLE AND LENTIL SALAD WITH PINE NUT CREAM

Prep Time: 20 minutes | **Cook Time:** 30 minutes | **Servings:** 4

Ingredients:

For the Salad:

- 1 cup green or brown lentils, rinsed and drained
- 4 cups mixed fall vegetables (e.g., butternut squash, Brussels sprouts, carrots), peeled and chopped into bite-sized pieces
- 2 tablespoons olive oil
- Salt and black pepper to taste
- 1/4 cup dried cranberries
- 1/4 cup chopped fresh parsley
- 1/4 cup chopped fresh sage leaves
- 1/4 cup chopped pecans, toasted (optional)

For the Pine Nut Cream:

- 1/2 cup pine nuts, toasted
- 2 tablespoons fresh lemon juice

- 2 tablespoons extra-virgin olive oil
- 1 small garlic clove, minced
- Salt and black pepper to taste
- Water, as needed to adjust consistency

Instructions:

<u>For the Salad:</u>

1. **Preheat the Oven:** Preheat your oven to 425°F (220°C).
2. **Roast Vegetables:** In a large bowl, toss the chopped fall vegetables with olive oil, salt, and black pepper. Spread them in a single layer on a baking sheet. Bake in the hot oven for 25-30 minutes | or until the vegetables are soft and slightly browned.
3. **Cook Lentils:** Bring 4 cups of water to a boil in a medium saucepan while the vegetables roast. Add the rinsed lentils and reduce the heat to a simmer. Cook for about 20-25 minutes | or until the lentils are tender but still hold their shape. Drain any excess water.
4. **Combine Ingredients:** In a large bowl, combine the roasted fall vegetables, cooked lentils, dried cranberries, chopped parsley, chopped sage, and toasted pecans (if using). Toss gently to mix.

<u>For the Pine Nut Cream:</u>

1. **Prepare Pine Nut Cream:** In a blender or food processor, combine the toasted pine nuts, fresh lemon juice, extra-virgin olive oil, minced garlic, salt, and black pepper. Blend until you achieve a creamy consistency. If the cream is too thick, add water to reach your desired consistency.

<u>To Serve:</u>

1. **Plate the Salad:** Divide the fall roasted vegetable and lentil salad among serving plates.
2. **Drizzle with Pine Nut Cream:** Drizzle the pine nut cream over the salad.
3. **Garnish:** Garnish with additional chopped herbs or toasted pecans if desired.
4. **Serve:** Serve the Fall Roasted Vegetable and Lentil Salad with Pine Nut Cream as a hearty and flavorful Mediterranean-inspired dish.

Nutrition Information (per serving):

- Calories: 385 kcal
- Protein: 12g
- Carbohydrates: 44g
- Dietary Fiber: 13g

- Sugars: 9g
- Fat: 20g
- Saturated Fat: 2g
- Cholesterol: 0mg
- Sodium: 24mg
- Potassium: 886mg

SKILLET CHICKEN FAJITAS

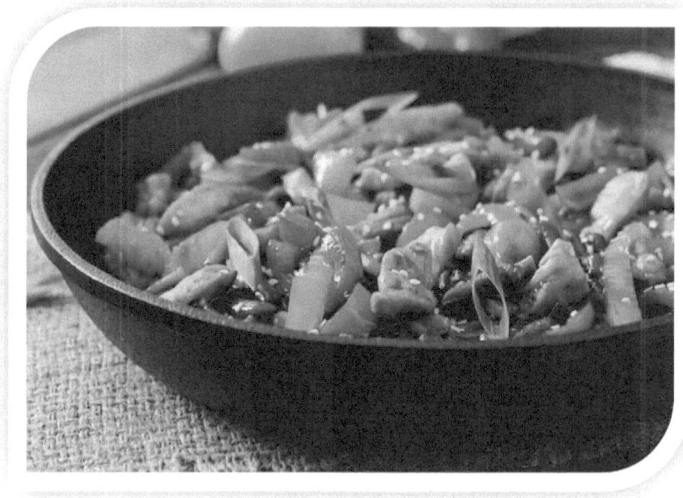

Prep Time: 15 minutes | **Cook Time:** 15 minutes | **Servings:** 4

Ingredients:

For the Chicken Marinade:

- One pound of chicken breasts without bones or skin, cut into thin pieces.
- 2 tablespoons olive oil
- 2 cloves garlic, minced
- 1 teaspoon chili powder
- 1 teaspoon ground cumin
- 1/2 teaspoon paprika
- Salt and black pepper to taste
- Juice of 1 lime

For the Fajita Veggies:

- 1 red bell pepper, thinly sliced
- 1 green bell pepper, thinly sliced
- 1 yellow onion, thinly sliced
- 1 tablespoon olive oil

- Salt and black pepper to taste

For Serving:

- 8 small whole wheat or corn tortillas
- Sour cream or Greek yogurt (optional)
- Salsa (optional)
- Fresh cilantro leaves (optional)
- Lime wedges (optional)

Instructions:

For the Chicken Marinade:

1. **Marinate Chicken:** In a bowl, combine the sliced chicken breasts with olive oil, minced garlic, chili powder, ground cumin, paprika, salt, black pepper, and lime juice. Toss to coat the chicken evenly. Allow it to marinate for at least 15 minutes.

For the Fajita Veggies:

2. **Sauté Veggies:** Heat olive oil over medium-high heat in a large skillet. Add the sliced red and green bell peppers and the thinly sliced yellow onion. Sauté for about 5-7 minutes | or until the veggies are tender and slightly caramelized. Add some salt and black pepper until it tastes good to you. Take out of the frying pan and keep to the side.

For the Chicken:

3. **Cook Chicken:** In the same skillet, add the marinated chicken slices. Cook the chicken for 5-7 minutes | or until it is fully cooked and has a nice brown crust on the outside.

To Serve:

4. **Warm Tortillas:** While cooking the chicken, heat the tortillas in a different pan or microwave until they are warm.
5. **Assemble Fajitas:** Place a spoonful of the cooked chicken on a tortilla, followed by a portion of the sautéed bell peppers and onions to assemble the fajitas. Add sour cream or Greek yogurt, salsa, and fresh cilantro leaves.
6. **Garnish:** Serve the Skillet Chicken Fajitas with lime wedges for squeezing over the top.

Nutrition Information (per serving, 2 fajitas):

- Calories: 367 kcal
- Protein: 25g
- Carbohydrates: 33g
- Dietary Fiber: 6g
- Sugars: 4g
- Fat: 14g
- Saturated Fat: 2g
- Cholesterol: 63mg
- Sodium: 437mg
- Potassium: 587mg

PASTA PUTTANESCA

Prep Time: 10 minutes | **Cook Time:** 20 minutes | **Servings:** 4

Ingredients:

- 12 ounces (about 340g) of spaghetti or linguine
- 2 tablespoons olive oil
- 4 cloves garlic, minced
- 2 anchovy fillets (optional for added depth of flavor)
- Use a little red pepper flakes, about 1/4 of a teaspoon. You can add more or less depending on how spicy you like it.
- 1 can (14 ounces) diced tomatoes
- 1/4 cup pitted Kalamata olives, chopped
- 2 tablespoons capers, drained
- 2 tablespoons fresh parsley, chopped

- Salt and black pepper to taste
- Grated Parmesan cheese (optional for serving)

Instructions:

1. **Cook Pasta:** Cook the spaghetti or linguine according to package instructions until al dente. Drain and set aside.
2. **Prepare the Sauce:** Warm the olive oil in a big frying pan on medium heat. Add the minced garlic and anchovy fillets (if using). Sauté for about 1-2 minutes | until the garlic is fragrant and the anchovies have melted into the oil.
3. **Add Red Pepper Flakes and Tomatoes:** Stir in the red pepper flakes and canned diced tomatoes. Warm the sauce until it makes small bubbles, and let it cook for around 10 minutes | so it becomes a little thicker.
4. **Incorporate Olives and Capers:** Add the chopped Kalamata olives and drained capers to the sauce. Simmer for an additional 5 minutes, allowing the flavors to meld together.
5. **Season and Toss:** Taste the sauce and season with salt and black pepper as needed. Remember that the olives and capers add saltiness, so adjust accordingly.
6. **Combine with Pasta:** Add the cooked pasta to the skillet with the sauce. Toss everything together to ensure the pasta is well coated in the flavorful puttanesca sauce.
7. **Serve:** Divide the Pasta Puttanesca among four serving plates. Sprinkle chopped fresh parsley over each portion. If desired, top with grated Parmesan cheese.

Nutrition Information (per serving):

- Calories: 316 kcal
- Protein: 8g
- Carbohydrates: 50g
- Dietary Fiber: 5g
- Sugars: 3g
- Fat: 9g
- Saturated Fat: 1g
- Cholesterol: 0mg
- Sodium: 587mg
- Potassium: 362mg

CHICKEN MEATBALLS WITH GREEK YOGURT AND QUINOA

Prep Time: 15 minutes | **Cook Time:** 20 minutes | **Servings:** 4

Ingredients:

For the Chicken Meatballs:

- 1 pound ground chicken
- 1/2 cup breadcrumbs
- 1/4 cup grated Parmesan cheese
- 1/4 cup finely chopped fresh parsley
- 1/4 cup finely chopped red onion
- 2 cloves garlic, minced
- 1 egg
- 1/2 teaspoon dried oregano

- Salt and black pepper to taste
- 2 tablespoons olive oil, for cooking

For the Greek Yogurt Sauce:

- 1 cup Greek yogurt
- 1 tablespoon fresh lemon juice
- 1 teaspoon fresh dill, chopped
- Salt and black pepper to taste

For the Quinoa:

- 1 cup quinoa, rinsed and drained
- 2 cups water
- Salt to taste

Instructions:

For the Chicken Meatballs:

1. **Prepare Chicken Mixture:** In a large mixing bowl, combine the ground chicken, breadcrumbs, grated Parmesan cheese, chopped parsley, chopped red onion, minced garlic, egg, dried oregano, salt, and black pepper. Mix until all the ingredients are well combined.
2. **Shape Meatballs:** Using your hands, shape the mixture into small meatballs, about 1 to 1.5 inches in diameter. You should have approximately 16 meatballs.
3. **Cook Meatballs:** Heat the olive oil over medium-high heat in a large skillet. Add the meatballs and cook for 4-5 minutes | per side until they are browned on the outside and cooked through. Ensure they get cooked until they are 165°F (74°C) inside. Remove the meatballs from the skillet and set them aside.

For the Greek Yogurt Sauce:

4. **Prepare Yogurt Sauce:** In a bowl, combine the Greek yogurt, fresh lemon juice, chopped dill, salt, and black pepper. Mix until well blended. Adjust the seasoning to taste.

For the Quinoa:

5. **Cook Quinoa:** Combine the rinsed quinoa and water in a separate saucepan. Add a pinch of salt. Heat the mixture until it starts bubbling, then lower the heat and cover it. Let it cook slowly for around 15 minutes | until the quinoa is cooked and the water is absorbed. Fluff with a fork.

<u>To Serve:</u>

6. **Plate the Dish:** Divide the cooked quinoa among serving plates. Top with the chicken meatballs and drizzle with the Greek yogurt sauce.
7. **Garnish:** Garnish with additional chopped fresh dill or parsley if desired.

Nutrition Information (per serving):

- Calories: 476 kcal
- Protein: 34g
- Carbohydrates: 36g
- Dietary Fiber: 4g
- Sugars: 4g
- Fat: 20g
- Saturated Fat: 5g
- Cholesterol: 142mg
- Sodium: 411mg
- Potassium: 564mg

PASTA ALLA NORMA

Prep Time: 15 minutes | **Cook Time:** 30 minutes | **Servings:** 4

Ingredients:

- 12 ounces (about 340g) pasta (spaghetti or penne work well)
- 2 large eggplants (aubergines), diced into small cubes
- 1/4 cup olive oil
- 3 cloves garlic, minced
- 1 can (14 ounces) diced tomatoes
- Use a small amount of red pepper flakes, about 1/4 of a teaspoon, and adjust the amount according to your preference for spiciness.
- Salt and black pepper to taste
- 1/2 cup fresh basil leaves, torn or chopped
- 1/2 cup grated ricotta salata cheese (or substitute with grated Parmesan)
- Extra fresh basil leaves for garnish (optional)

Instructions:

1. **Roast the Eggplant:**
   - Preheat your oven to 400°F (200°C).
   - Place the diced eggplant cubes on a baking sheet. Drizzle with 2 tablespoons of olive oil and season with salt and black pepper. Toss to coat evenly.

- Roast in the oven for about 20-25 minutes | or until the eggplant is tender and golden brown. Remove from the oven and set aside.

2. **Cook the Pasta:**
    - While the eggplant is roasting, bring a large pot of salted water to a boil. Boil the pasta until it is cooked but still firm. Follow the instructions on the package. Empty and put aside.

3. **Prepare the Sauce:**
    - Warm up the rest of the 2 tablespoons of olive oil on medium heat in a big frying pan. Put in the chopped garlic and red pepper flakes. Cook in a hot pan for about 1 minute until it smells nice.
    - Add the canned diced tomatoes (with their juice) to the skillet. Cook for about 10-12 minutes, allowing the sauce to thicken. Season with salt and black pepper to taste.

4. **Combine Pasta and Eggplant:**
    - Add the roasted eggplant cubes to the tomato sauce and toss to combine. Keep cooking for another 2-3 minutes | until it is heated completely.

5. **Toss with Basil:**
    - Take the pan off the stove and mix in ripped or cut fresh basil leaves.

6. **Serve:**
    - Divide the cooked pasta among serving plates. Spoon the Eggplant and Tomato sauce over the pasta.
    - Top with grated ricotta salata cheese or Parmesan.
    - Garnish with extra fresh basil leaves if desired.

Nutrition Information (per serving):

- Calories: 392 kcal
- Protein: 10g
- Carbohydrates: 59g
- Dietary Fiber: 9g
- Sugars: 7g
- Fat: 14g
- Saturated Fat: 2g
- Cholesterol: 4mg
- Sodium: 120mg
- Potassium: 761mg

FREEKEH VEGETABLE SOUP

Prep Time: 15 minutes | **Cook Time:** 45 minutes | **Servings:** 4

Ingredients:

- 1 cup cracked freekeh
- 1 tablespoon olive oil
- 1 onion, diced
- 2 carrots, diced
- 2 celery stalks, diced
- 2 cloves garlic, minced
- 1 teaspoon ground cumin
- 1 teaspoon ground coriander
- 1/2 teaspoon turmeric
- 1/2 teaspoon paprika
- 1/4 teaspoon red pepper flakes (adjust to taste)
- 6 cups vegetable broth
- 1 can (14 ounces) diced tomatoes
- 2 bay leaves
- Salt and black pepper to taste

- 2 cups chopped spinach or kale
- Juice of 1 lemon
- Fresh parsley or cilantro for garnish (optional)

Instructions:

1. **Rinse and Drain Freekeh:**
    - Place the cracked freekeh in a fine-mesh strainer and rinse it under cold running water. Drain and set aside.
2. **Sauté Vegetables:**
    - In a large pot, heat the olive oil over medium heat. Add the diced onion, carrots, and celery. Sauté for about 5-7 minutes | or until the vegetables soften.
3. **Add Spices:**
    - Stir in the minced garlic, ground cumin, coriander, turmeric, paprika, and red pepper flakes. Cook for an additional 1-2 minutes | until fragrant.
4. **Combine Broth and Tomatoes:**
    - Pour the vegetable broth and add the diced tomatoes (with their juice) to the pot. Stir to combine.
5. **Simmer Soup:**
    - Add the rinsed and drained cracked freekeh and bay leaves to the soup. Begin by heating the mixture until it bubbles, then lower the temperature and cover it. Let it cook gently for about half an hour to thirty-five minutes | or until the freekeh is soft.
6. **Season and Add Greens:**
    - Remove the bay leaves from the soup. Sprinkle salt and black pepper on your food until it tastes good.
    - Stir in the chopped spinach or kale and cook for 2-3 minutes | until wilted.
7. **Finish with Lemon Juice:**
    - Squeeze the juice of one lemon into the soup. Stir to combine.
8. **Serve:**
    - Ladle the Freekeh Vegetable Soup into bowls. Add fresh parsley or cilantro on top if you want.

Nutrition Information (per serving):

- Calories: 310 kcal
- Protein: 12g
- Carbohydrates: 59g
- Dietary Fiber: 11g
- Sugars: 8g

- Fat: 5g
- Saturated Fat: 1g
- Cholesterol: 0mg
- Sodium: 1257mg
- Potassium: 628mg

CREAMY MEDITERRANEAN CHICKEN

Prep Time: 15 minutes | **Cook Time:** 25 minutes | **Servings:** 4

Ingredients:

- 4 boneless, skinless chicken breasts
- Salt and black pepper to taste
- 2 tablespoons olive oil
- 1 onion, finely chopped
- 3 cloves garlic, minced
- 1 can (14 ounces) diced tomatoes
- 1/2 cup pitted Kalamata olives, sliced
- 1/4 cup sun-dried tomatoes, chopped
- 1 teaspoon dried oregano
- 1/2 teaspoon dried basil
- 1/2 teaspoon dried thyme
- 1/2 cup heavy cream
- 1/2 cup crumbled feta cheese
- Fresh parsley for garnish (optional)

Instructions:

1. **Season and Sear Chicken:**
   - Put salt and black pepper on both sides of the chicken breasts. Warm up the olive oil in a big frying pan on medium to high heat. Put the chicken breasts in the pan and cook them on each side for 4-5 minutes | until they turn golden brown and are fully cooked. Take out the chicken from the pan and keep it to the side.

2. **Sauté Onions and Garlic:**
   - In the same skillet, add the finely chopped onion and minced garlic. Sauté for about 2-3 minutes | until the onions become translucent.

3. **Add Tomatoes and Herbs:**
   - Stir in the diced tomatoes, Kalamata olives, chopped sun-dried tomatoes, dried oregano, dried basil, and dried thyme. Cook the food for 3-4 minutes | to blend the flavors well.

4. **Pour in Cream and Feta:**
   - Reduce the heat to low, and pour in the heavy cream. Stir to combine. Put the broken feta cheese into the mixture and keep stirring until the cheese becomes liquid in the sauce.

5. **Return Chicken to Skillet:**
   - Put the chicken back into the skillet and place it in the creamy Mediterranean sauce.

6. **Simmer and Serve:**
   - Put a lid on the pan and cook for 5-7 minutes | until the chicken is hot and the sauce gets thicker.

7. **Garnish and Serve:**
   - Garnish with fresh parsley if desired.

Nutrition Information (per serving):

- Calories: 423 kcal
- Protein: 32g
- Carbohydrates: 11g
- Dietary Fiber: 2g
- Sugars: 4g
- Fat: 29g
- Saturated Fat: 12g
- Cholesterol: 130mg
- Sodium: 967mg
- Potassium: 874mg

PAN-FRIED COD WITH ORANGE AND SWISS CHARD

Prep Time: 15 minutes | **Cook Time:** 15 minutes | **Servings:** 4

Ingredients:

- 4 cod fillets (about 6 ounces each)
- Salt and black pepper to taste
- 2 tablespoons olive oil
- 1 onion, thinly sliced
- 2 cloves garlic, minced
- 4 cups Swiss chard, stems removed and leaves chopped
- Zest and juice of 1 orange
- 1/4 cup chicken or vegetable broth
- 1/4 cup dry white wine (optional)
- 2 tablespoons fresh parsley, chopped
- Orange slices for garnish (optional)

Instructions:

1. **Season the Cod:**
   - Season the cod fillets with salt and black pepper on both sides.
2. **Sear the Cod:**

- Warm up the olive oil in a big frying pan on medium to high heat. Put the cod pieces into the frying pan and cook them on each side for about 3 to 4 minutes. Keep cooking until they turn opaque and can be easily separated with a fork. Remove the cod from the skillet and set it aside.

3. **Sauté Onions and Garlic:**
   - Put the thinly cut onion and chopped garlic in the same frying pan. Sauté for about 2-3 minutes | until the onions become translucent.

4. **Add Swiss Chard:**
   - Add the chopped Swiss chard leaves to the pan and cook for 3-4 minutes | until they become soft and tender.

5. **Create the Sauce:**
   - Add the orange zest, orange juice, chicken or vegetable broth, and white wine (if using). Stir to combine. Slowly cook the food on low heat for 3-4 minutes | to mix the flavors and make the sauce thicker.

6. **Return Cod to Skillet:**
   - Return the seared cod fillets to the skillet, nestling them into the Swiss chard and sauce.

7. **Finish and Garnish:**
   - Sprinkle fresh parsley over the top. Garnish with orange slices if desired.

Nutrition Information (per serving):

- Calories: 253 kcal
- Protein: 27g
- Carbohydrates: 10g
- Dietary Fiber: 2g
- Sugars: 3g
- Fat: 10g
- Saturated Fat: 2g
- Cholesterol: 64mg
- Sodium: 341mg
- Potassium: 883mg

LAMB MEATBALL AND ESCAROLE SOUP

Prep Time: 20 minutes | **Cook Time:** 30 minutes | **Servings:** 4

Ingredients:

For the Lamb Meatballs:

- 1 pound ground lamb
- 1/4 cup breadcrumbs
- 1/4 cup grated Parmesan cheese
- 1/4 cup finely chopped fresh parsley
- 1 egg
- 2 cloves garlic, minced
- Salt and black pepper to taste

For the Soup:

- 2 tablespoons olive oil
- 1 onion, finely chopped
- 2 carrots, diced
- 2 celery stalks, diced
- 2 cloves garlic, minced
- 8 cups chicken or vegetable broth

- 1 head escarole, chopped
- 1/2 cup orzo pasta
- Salt and black pepper to taste
- Fresh lemon juice (from 1 lemon)

Instructions:

Prepare the Lamb Meatballs:

1. Combine the ground lamb, breadcrumbs, grated Parmesan cheese, chopped fresh parsley, egg, minced garlic, salt, and black pepper in a large mixing bowl. Mix until well combined.
2. Make small round balls from the mixture, each about 1 inch wide.

Sear the Lamb Meatballs:

3. In a large pot, heat the olive oil over medium-high heat. Add the lamb meatballs and sear them on all sides until they are browned. Remove the meatballs from the pot and set them aside.

Sauté Vegetables:

4. Put the chopped onion, carrots, and celery into the pot. Sauté for about 5 minutes | or until the vegetables begin to soften.
5. Add minced garlic and sauté for 1-2 minutes | until fragrant.

Simmer Soup:

6. Add the chicken or vegetable liquid and wait until it begins to boil.
7. Add the chopped escarole and orzo pasta to the pot. Turn the heat down and let it cook gently for 10-12 minutes | or until the orzo is soft.

Return Meatballs and Season:

8. Return the seared lamb meatballs to the soup and simmer for 5-7 minutes | or until the meatballs are cooked through.
9. Add salt and black pepper to the soup until it tastes good.

Finish and Serve:

10. Squeeze fresh lemon juice into the soup, stirring to combine.
11. Ladle the Lamb Meatball and Escarole Soup into serving bowls.

Nutrition Information (per serving):

- Calories: 527 kcal
- Protein: 28g
- Carbohydrates: 29g
- Dietary Fiber: 6g
- Sugars: 6g
- Fat: 35g
- Saturated Fat: 13g
- Cholesterol: 135mg
- Sodium: 1458mg
- Potassium: 1216mg

SHRIMP WITH CAULIFLOWER "GRITS" AND ARUGULA

Prep Time: 20 minutes | **Cook Time:** 20 minutes | **Servings:** 4

Ingredients:

For the Shrimp:

- 1 pound large shrimp, peeled and deveined
- 2 tablespoons olive oil
- 2 cloves garlic, minced
- 1 teaspoon paprika
- Use a little red pepper flakes (adjust the amount to your preference) - about half a teaspoon.
- Salt and black pepper to taste
- Juice of 1 lemon
- Fresh parsley for garnish

For the Cauliflower "Grits":

- 1 large head cauliflower, cut into florets
- 2 tablespoons butter

- 1/4 cup grated Parmesan cheese
- Salt and black pepper to taste

For the Arugula Salad:

- 4 cups fresh arugula leaves
- 2 tablespoons olive oil
- Juice of 1 lemon
- Salt and black pepper to taste

Instructions:

Prepare the Shrimp:

1. Mix the shrimp, garlic, paprika, red pepper flakes, salt, black pepper, and lemon juice in a bowl. Sprinkle the shrimp with a little coating to ensure it is spread evenly on them.
2. Heat 2 tablespoons of olive oil in a large skillet over medium-high heat. Put the shrimp in the pan and cook them for 2-3 minutes | on each side until they turn pink and you can't see through them. Take the cooked shrimp from the skillet and put them to the side.

Make the Cauliflower "Grits":

3. Use a food processor machine to chop up the cauliflower to look like little pieces of rice.
4. Heat the butter in a big frying pan on medium heat until it becomes liquid. Put the cauliflower into the pan and cook it for 5-7 minutes | or until it becomes soft.
5. Mix in the shredded Parmesan cheese, and add salt and black pepper to your liking. Stay cozy

Prepare the Arugula Salad:

6. Combine the fresh arugula leaves with 2 tablespoons of olive oil and the juice from one lemon in a bowl. Put as much salt and black pepper as you want.

Serve:

7. To serve, spoon a portion of the cauliflower "grits" onto each plate, top with the cooked shrimp, and garnish with fresh parsley.
8. Serve alongside the arugula salad.

Nutrition Information (per serving):

- Calories: 298 kcal
- Protein: 27g
- Carbohydrates: 15g
- Dietary Fiber: 6g
- Sugars: 4g
- Fat: 15g
- Saturated Fat: 5g
- Cholesterol: 228mg
- Sodium: 473mg
- Potassium: 889mg

CHICKPEA SHAWARMA SALAD

Prep Time: 15 minutes | **Cook Time:** 10 minutes | (optional for warming chickpeas) **Servings:** 4

Ingredients:

<u>For the Chickpeas:</u>

- You need 2 cans of chickpeas, each weighing 15 ounces. Make sure to remove the liquid and clean the chickpeas before using them.
- 2 tablespoons olive oil
- 2 teaspoons ground cumin
- 1 teaspoon ground paprika
- 1/2 teaspoon ground turmeric
- 1/2 teaspoon ground cinnamon
- Salt and black pepper to taste

<u>For the Salad:</u>

- 4 cups mixed greens (e.g., lettuce, spinach, arugula)

- 1 cucumber, diced
- 1 cup cherry tomatoes, halved
- 1/2 red onion, thinly sliced
- 1/4 cup fresh parsley, chopped

For the Tahini Dressing:

- 1/4 cup tahini
- 2 tablespoons lemon juice
- 2 tablespoons water
- 2 cloves garlic, minced
- 1/2 teaspoon ground cumin
- Salt and black pepper to taste

Instructions:

Prepare the Chickpeas:

1. Heat 2 tablespoons of olive oil in a big pan on medium heat. Put the drained chickpeas in.
2. Sprinkle ground cumin, paprika, turmeric, cinnamon, salt, and black pepper over the chickpeas. Stir well to coat the chickpeas evenly with the spices.
3. Sauté the chickpeas for about 5-7 minutes | until they are heated and slightly crispy. Remove from heat and set aside.

Make the Tahini Dressing:

4. Mix tahini, lemon juice, water, minced garlic, ground cumin, salt, and black pepper until smooth. Add more water if you need to make it thinner.

Assemble the Salad:

5. Combine the mixed greens, diced cucumber, halved cherry tomatoes, thinly sliced red onion, and fresh parsley in a large salad bowl.
6. Drizzle the tahini dressing over the salad ingredients and toss to combine.
7. Top the salad with the sautéed chickpeas.

Serve:

8. Divide the Chickpea Shawarma Salad among four plates and serve immediately.

Nutrition Information (per serving):

- Calories: 378 kcal
- Protein: 12g
- Carbohydrates: 38g
- Dietary Fiber: 10g
- Sugars: 6g
- Fat: 22g
- Saturated Fat: 3g
- Cholesterol: 0mg
- Sodium: 282mg
- Potassium: 670mg

CORN AND TOMATO SALAD WITH FETA AND LIME

Prep Time: 15 minutes | **Cook Time:** 5 minutes | (optional for blanching corn) **Servings:** 4

Ingredients:

- 4 fresh corn on the cob, with the leaves and seeds taken off (approximately 4 cups)
- 1 pint cherry tomatoes, halved
- 1/2 red onion, finely chopped
- 1/2 cup crumbled feta cheese
- Use 1/4 cup of either fresh cilantro or parsley that has been chopped.
- Zest and juice of 2 limes
- 2 tablespoons extra-virgin olive oil
- Salt and black pepper to taste
- Red pepper flakes (optional for added heat)

Instructions:

<u>Blanch the Corn (Optional):</u>

1. If desired, bring a large pot of water to a boil. Add the corn kernels and blanch them for about 2-3 minutes. Pour the liquid out and put it in a bowl of icy water to cool down. Drain once more and keep it aside.

<u>Prepare the Salad:</u>

2. Combine the blanched corn kernels (if using), cherry tomato halves, finely chopped red onion, and crumbled feta cheese in a large salad bowl.
3. In a little bowl, mix the grated outer part and the liquid from 2 limes, a type of healthy olive oil, salt, black pepper, and red pepper flakes (if you want it a little spicy).
4. Drizzle the lime dressing over the salad ingredients.
5. Mix the ingredients in the salad gently so they are well combined and covered with dressing evenly.

<u>Chill and Serve:</u>

6. Put the Corn and Tomato Salad in the refrigerator for around 30 minutes | to let the flavors mix.
7. Just before serving, sprinkle fresh cilantro or parsley over the top as a garnish.

Nutrition Information (per serving):

- Calories: 255 kcal
- Protein: 7g
- Carbohydrates: 32g
- Dietary Fiber: 4g
- Sugars: 9g
- Fat: 13g
- Saturated Fat: 4g
- Cholesterol: 17mg
- Sodium: 309mg
- Potassium: 507mg

SLOW COOKER PASTA E FAGIOLI SOUP

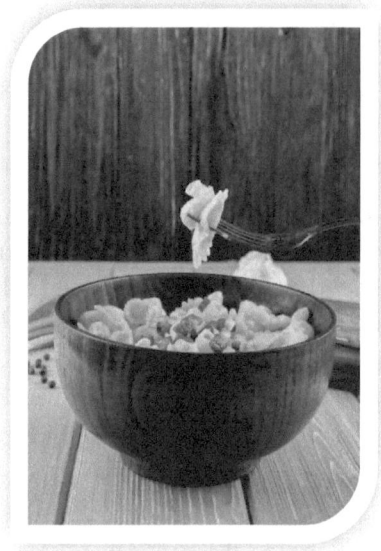

Prep Time: 15 minutes | **Cook Time:** 4-6 hours (slow cooker) **Servings:** 6

Ingredients:

- One pound of ground beef (or ground turkey if you prefer a healthier choice)
- 1 onion, chopped
- 2 carrots, diced
- 2 celery stalks, diced
- 3 cloves garlic, minced
- Take one can of red kidney beans, which weigh 15 ounces, and remove any liquid by draining them. Rinse the beans with water before using them.
- 1 can (15 ounces) cannellini beans, drained and rinsed
- 2 cans (14.5 ounces each) diced tomatoes
- 1 can (15 ounces) tomato sauce
- 4 cups beef broth (or vegetable broth)
- 1 teaspoon dried oregano
- 1 teaspoon dried basil
- Use half a teaspoon of red pepper flakes, and change the amount if you want more or less spiciness.

- Salt and black pepper to taste
- 1 cup ditalini pasta (or small pasta of your choice)
- Fresh parsley, chopped, for garnish
- Grated Parmesan cheese for serving

Instructions:

1. In a big pan, cook the beef on medium-high heat until it turns brown. Break the food into small pieces while it is cooking. Remove any extra grease or oil.
2. Transfer the cooked beef to your slow cooker.
3. Add the chopped onion to the slow cooker, diced carrots, diced celery, minced garlic, drained and rinsed red kidney beans, drained and rinsed cannellini beans, diced tomatoes, tomato sauce, beef broth, dried oregano, dried basil, black pepper, red pepper flakes, and salt. Stir well to combine.
4. Cover the slow cooker and cook on LOW for 4-6 hours or until the vegetables are tender.
5. About 30 minutes | before serving, stir in the ditalini pasta. Continue cooking until the pasta is tender.
6. Try the soup; add extra salt and pepper if it needs more flavor.
7. Serve the food hot, and add some chopped fresh parsley and grated Parmesan cheese on top.

Nutrition Information (per serving):

- Calories: 369 kcal
- Protein: 26g
- Carbohydrates: 48g
- Dietary Fiber: 10g
- Sugars: 7g
- Fat: 9g
- Saturated Fat: 3g
- Cholesterol: 40mg
- Sodium: 1045mg
- Potassium: 1021mg

GRILLED CAPRESE SKEWERS

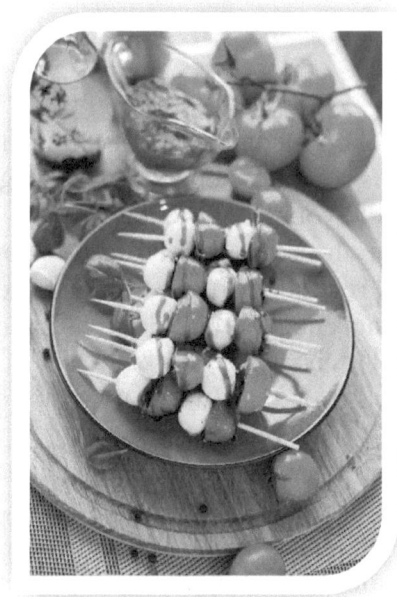

Prep Time: 15 minutes | **Cook Time:** 5 minutes | (grilling time) **Servings:** 4

Ingredients:

- 12 cherry tomatoes
- 12 fresh mozzarella balls
- 12 fresh basil leaves
- 2 tablespoons extra-virgin olive oil
- 1 tablespoon balsamic vinegar (optional)
- Salt and black pepper to taste
- Soak the wooden sticks in water for 30 minutes | to stop them from getting burned.

Instructions:

1. Preheat your grill to medium-high heat.
2. Thread one cherry tomato, mozzarella ball, and basil leaf onto each skewer, repeating until you have 12 skewers.
3. Mix the olive oil and balsamic vinegar (if you have it). Put salt and black pepper into the mixture as much as you like.

4. Brush the skewers with the olive oil and balsamic mixture on all sides.
5. Place the skewers on the preheated grill and cook on each side for 2-3 minutes | until the tomatoes are slightly blistered and the mozzarella melts.
6. Take the sticks out from the grill and move them onto a plate for serving.
7. Put olive oil and balsamic mixture on the skewers to make them taste better.
8. Serve the Grilled Caprese Skewers immediately as a delightful appetizer or side dish.

Nutrition Information (per serving - 3 skewers):

- Calories: 165 kcal
- Protein: 9g
- Carbohydrates: 4g
- Dietary Fiber: 1g
- Sugars: 2g
- Fat: 13g
- Saturated Fat: 5g
- Cholesterol: 25mg
- Sodium: 185mg
- Potassium: 152mg

MEDITERRANEAN GRILLED VEGETABLES

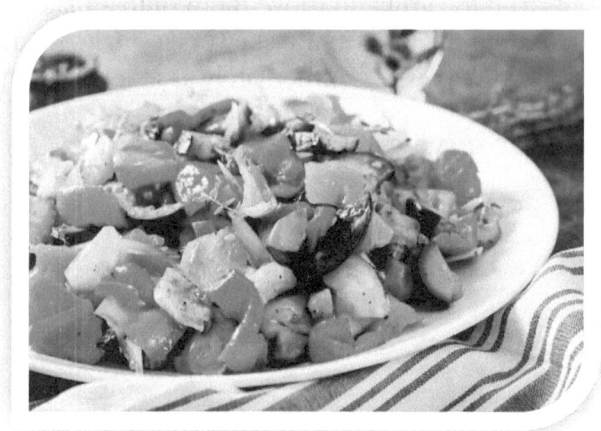

Prep Time: 15 minutes | **Grilling Time:** 10-15 minutes | **Servings:** 4

Ingredients:

- 2 zucchinis, sliced lengthwise into 1/4-inch thick strips
- 2 red bell peppers, cut into large chunks
- 2 yellow bell peppers, cut into large chunks
- 1 red onion, cut into thick slices
- 1 eggplant, sliced into rounds or lengthwise strips
- 2 tablespoons extra-virgin olive oil
- 2 cloves garlic, minced
- 2 teaspoons dried oregano
- Salt and black pepper to taste
- Juice of 1 lemon
- Fresh basil leaves for garnish (optional)

Instructions:

Prepare the Vegetables:

1. Preheat your grill to medium-high heat.
2. Combine the zucchini slices, red bell pepper chunks, yellow bell pepper chunks, red onion slices, and eggplant slices in a large bowl.

3. Mix the olive oil, garlic, oregano, salt, pepper, and lemon juice in a small bowl.
4. Pour the olive oil mixture over the vegetables and mix them well until they are evenly coated.

Grill the Vegetables:

5. Put the marinated vegetables on skewers or use a grill basket to stop them from falling on the grill.
6. Place the vegetable skewers or grill basket on the preheated grill.
7. Grill the vegetables for 10-15 minutes, occasionally turning, until they are tender and have grill marks.

Serve:

8. Move the grilled vegetables to a dish, decorate with basil leaves if wanted, and serve while still warm.

Nutrition Information (per serving):

- Calories: 143 kcal
- Protein: 3g
- Carbohydrates: 21g
- Dietary Fiber: 7g
- Sugars: 10g
- Fat: 7g
- Saturated Fat: 1g
- Cholesterol: 0mg
- Sodium: 10mg
- Potassium: 669mg

GRILLED BROCCOLI RABE

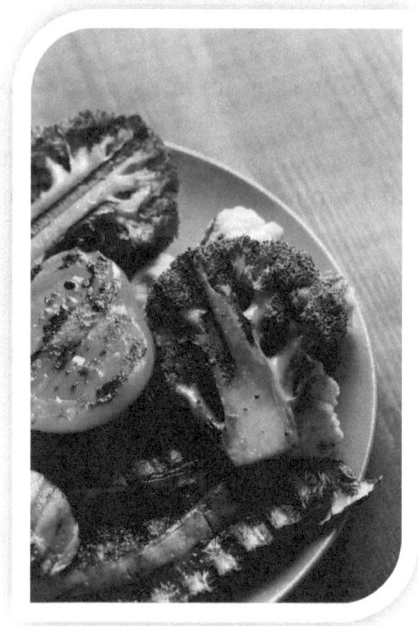

Prep Time: 10 minutes | **Grilling Time:** 8-10 minutes | **Servings:** 4

Ingredients:

- 1 bunch broccoli rabe (rapini), ends trimmed
- 2 tablespoons extra-virgin olive oil
- 3 cloves garlic, minced
- Red pepper flakes (optional for added heat)
- Salt and black pepper to taste
- Juice of 1 lemon
- Grated Parmesan cheese (optional for garnish)

Instructions:

Prepare the Broccoli Rabe:

1. Preheat your grill to medium-high heat.

2. In a large bowl, toss the trimmed broccoli rabe with 1 tablespoon of extra-virgin olive oil, minced garlic, and red pepper flakes (if using). Season with salt and black pepper to taste.

Grill the Broccoli Rabe:

3. Place the broccoli rabe directly on the grill grates. Grill 4-5 minutes | on each side or until the stalks are tender and slightly charred.
4. While grilling, occasionally drizzle the remaining 1 tablespoon of olive oil over the broccoli rabe to keep it moist and flavorful.

Serve:

5. Transfer the grilled broccoli rabe to a serving platter.
6. Squeeze the juice of a fresh lemon on top, and add grated Parmesan cheese if you want.
7. Serve the Grilled Broccoli Rabe hot as a delicious side dish or appetizer.

Nutrition Information (per serving):

1. Calories: 67 kcal
2. Protein: 3g
3. Carbohydrates: 4g
4. Dietary Fiber: 2g
5. Sugars: 0g
6. Fat: 5g
7. Saturated Fat: 1g
8. Cholesterol: 0mg
9. Sodium: 76mg
10. Potassium: 277mg

MEDITERRANEAN BAKED SWEET POTATOES

Prep Time: 15 minutes | **Baking Time:** 45-50 minutes | **Servings:** 4

Ingredients:

- 4 medium sweet potatoes
- One can of chickpeas (15 ounces) emptied of liquid and cleaned.
- 1 cup cherry tomatoes, halved
- 1/2 cucumber, diced
- 1/4 red onion, finely chopped
- 1/4 cup Kalamata olives, pitted and sliced
- 1/4 cup crumbled feta cheese
- 2 tablespoons extra-virgin olive oil
- 1 teaspoon dried oregano
- 1 teaspoon dried basil
- Salt and black pepper to taste
- Fresh parsley, chopped, for garnish (optional)

Instructions:

Bake the Sweet Potatoes:

1. Preheat your oven to 400°F (200°C).
2. Wash the sweet potatoes well and poke them with a fork a few times.
3. Put the sweet potatoes on a baking sheet and cook them in the oven for 45-50 minutes | until they are soft and can be poked easily with a knife.

Prepare the Mediterranean Topping:

4. Get the Mediterranean topping ready while the sweet potatoes are in the oven. Put the chickpeas, cherry tomatoes, cucumber, red onion, Kalamata olives, and feta cheese in a big bowl. Drizzle olive oil over the mixture and add dried oregano, basil, salt, and black pepper. Toss to combine all the ingredients evenly.

Assemble the Dish:

5. After the sweet potatoes finish baking, take them out of the oven and allow them to cool down a little bit.
6. Slice each sweet potato open lengthwise and fluff the flesh with a fork.
7. Spoon the Mediterranean topping generously onto each sweet potato.
8. Garnish with fresh chopped parsley, if desired.

Serve:

9. Serve the Mediterranean Baked Sweet Potatoes as a nutritious and delicious main dish or side.

Nutrition Information (per serving):

- Calories: 404 kcal
- Protein: 11g
- Carbohydrates: 69g
- Dietary Fiber: 11g
- Sugars: 14g
- Fat: 11g
- Saturated Fat: 2g
- Cholesterol: 6mg
- Sodium: 643mg
- Potassium: 1162mg

MEDITERRANEAN KALE

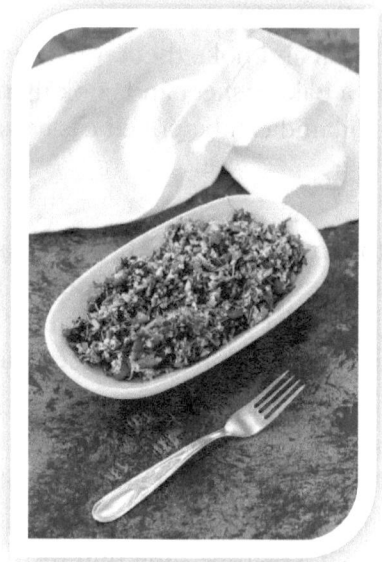

Prep Time: 10 minutes | **Cooking Time:** 10 minutes | **Servings:** 4

Ingredients:

- Take one bunch of kale and remove the stems. Then, chop up the leaves.
- 2 tablespoons extra-virgin olive oil
- 3 cloves garlic, minced
- You need one can of chickpeas that weighs 15 ounces. Make sure to drain and rinse the chickpeas before using them.
- 1/2 cup cherry tomatoes, halved
- 1/4 cup Kalamata olives, pitted and sliced
- 2 tablespoons crumbled feta cheese
- Juice of 1 lemon
- Salt and black pepper to taste
- Red pepper flakes (optional for added heat)
- Fresh parsley, chopped, for garnish (optional)

Instructions:

Prepare the Kale:

1. Wash the kale leaves thoroughly and remove the tough stems. Chop the leaves into bite-sized pieces.

Cook the Kale:

2. In a large skillet, heat the extra-virgin olive oil over medium heat.
3. Put the cut garlic in the pan and cook it for about 1 minute until it smells good.
4. Add the chopped kale to the skillet. Keep stirring and cook for 5-7 minutes | or until the kale is soft and tender.

Assemble the Dish:

5. Put the chickpeas, cherry tomatoes, Kalamata olives, and feta cheese into the same skillet as the cooked kale. Make sure to drain and rinse the chickpeas before adding.
6. Drizzle the lemon juice over the mixture and toss to combine all the ingredients.
7. Season it with salt and black pepper according to your preference. If you love spicy food, you can also add red pepper flakes.

Serve:

8. Transfer the Mediterranean Kale to a serving dish.
9. Garnish with fresh chopped parsley, if desired.

Nutrition Information (per serving):

- Calories: 199 kcal
- Protein: 7g
- Carbohydrates: 23g
- Dietary Fiber: 6g
- Sugars: 3g
- Fat: 9g
- Saturated Fat: 2g
- Cholesterol: 6mg
- Sodium: 442mg
- Potassium: 611mg

MEDITERRANEAN ZUCCHINI BOATS

Prep Time: 20 minutes | **Baking Time:** 25 minutes | **Servings:** 4

Ingredients:

- 4 medium zucchini
- 1 cup cooked quinoa
- 1 cup cherry tomatoes, diced
- 1/2 cup Kalamata olives, pitted and sliced
- 1/2 cup crumbled feta cheese
- 1/4 cup fresh basil leaves, chopped
- 2 cloves garlic, minced
- 2 tablespoons extra-virgin olive oil
- Juice of 1 lemon
- 1 teaspoon dried oregano
- Salt and black pepper to taste
- Red pepper flakes (optional for added heat)
- Fresh parsley, chopped, for garnish (optional)

Instructions:

Prepare the Zucchini Boats:

1. Preheat your oven to 375°F (190°C).

2. Cut the zucchini in half lengthwise. Scoop the flesh from the center of each zucchini half using a spoon, leaving about 1/4 inch of flesh along the edges. Reserve the scooped-out flesh.

Prepare the Filling:

3. Mix the cooked quinoa, diced cherry tomatoes, sliced Kalamata olives, crumbled feta cheese, and chopped fresh basil in a big bowl.
4. Combine minced garlic, olive oil, lemon juice, oregano, salt, and black pepper in a separate bowl. Mix ingredients to make a dressing.
5. Chop the reserved zucchini flesh and add it to the quinoa mixture.
6. Put the dressing on top of the quinoa mixture and mix it all. If you love spicy food, you can add red pepper flakes.

Fill the Zucchini Boats:

7. Put the zucchini boats in a baking dish.
8. Fill each zucchini boat with the quinoa and vegetable mixture, pressing it down slightly.

Bake:

9. Put aluminum foil on the baking dish and cook for 20-25 minutes | or until the zucchini is soft when poked with a fork.

Serve:

10. Garnish the Mediterranean Zucchini Boats with fresh chopped parsley if desired.
11. Serve hot as a delicious and nutritious main dish.

Nutrition Information (per serving):

- Calories: 264 kcal
- Protein: 8g
- Carbohydrates: 26g
- Dietary Fiber: 6g
- Sugars: 6g
- Fat: 15g
- Saturated Fat: 4g
- Cholesterol: 17mg
- Sodium: 687mg
- Potassium: 758mg

SICILIAN BLOOD ORANGE SALAD

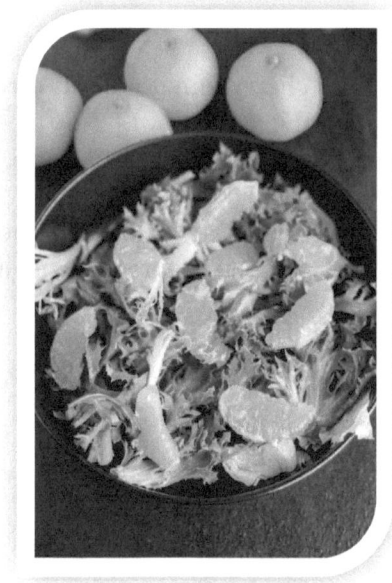

Prep Time: 15 minutes | Servings: 4

Ingredients:

- 4-5 blood oranges (you can also use regular oranges or a mix)
- 1 red onion, thinly sliced
- 1/4 cup Kalamata olives, pitted and sliced
- 2 tablespoons fresh mint leaves, chopped
- 2 tablespoons extra-virgin olive oil
- 1 tablespoon red wine vinegar
- Salt and black pepper to taste
- Crumbled feta cheese for garnish (optional)

Instructions:

Prepare the Blood Oranges:

1. Start by slicing off the tops and bottoms of the blood oranges to create flat surfaces. Then, use a sharp knife to remove the peel and pith from the oranges.

2. Slice the oranges crosswise into thin rounds or segments. Set aside.

Assemble the Salad:

3. In a big serving platter or bowl, arrange the sliced blood oranges.
4. Scatter the thinly sliced red onion over the oranges.
5. Sprinkle the Kalamata olives and chopped fresh mint leaves over the salad.

Make the Dressing:

6. Whisk the extra-virgin olive oil and red wine vinegar in a small bowl.
7. Drizzle the dressing over the salad.
8. Add salt and black pepper to taste.

Garnish and Serve:

9. Sprinkle crumbled feta cheese over the top of the salad for added flavor and creaminess.
10. Serve the Sicilian Blood Orange Salad immediately as a refreshing appetizer or side dish.

Nutrition Information (per serving):

- Calories: 120 kcal
- Protein: 1g
- Carbohydrates: 15g
- Dietary Fiber: 3g
- Sugars: 9g
- Fat: 7g
- Saturated Fat: 1g
- Cholesterol: 0mg
- Sodium: 152mg
- Potassium: 254mg

CHAPTER 5:
FLAVORFUL SIDES
AND SNACKS

THE BEST DRY-ROASTED CHICKPEAS

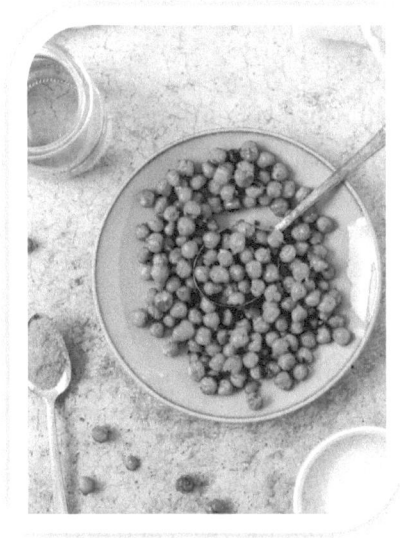

Prep Time: 10 minutes | **Baking Time:** 40 minutes | **Servings:** 4

Ingredients:

- 2 cans (15 ounces each) of chickpeas (garbanzo beans), drained and rinsed
- 2 tablespoons olive oil
- 1 teaspoon ground cumin
- 1 teaspoon smoked paprika
- 1/2 teaspoon garlic powder
- 1/2 teaspoon onion powder
- 1/2 teaspoon chili powder (adjust to taste for spiciness)
- Salt and black pepper to taste

Instructions:

Preheat the Oven:

1. Preheat your oven to 400°F (200°C) and line a baking sheet with parchment paper or a silicone mat.

<u>Dry Chickpeas:</u>

2. Drain and rinse the chickpeas thoroughly. Pat them dry with a clean kitchen towel or paper towel. Removing excess moisture will help them become crispy when roasted.

<u>Season the Chickpeas:</u>

3. Mix the dry chickpeas with olive oil, ground cumin, smoked paprika, garlic powder, onion powder, chili powder, salt, and black pepper in a big bowl. Mix the seasoning with the chickpeas until they are evenly coated.

<u>Roast the Chickpeas:</u>

4. Spread the seasoned chickpeas in a single layer on the prepared baking sheet.
5. Roast in the oven for about 40 minutes | or until the chickpeas are golden brown and crispy. Stir or shake the pan every 15 minutes | to ensure even roasting.

<u>Cool and Serve:</u>

6. Take the cooked chickpeas from the oven and allow them to cool a little.
7. Serve "The Best Dry-Roasted Chickpeas" as a crunchy and protein-packed snack. Enjoy!

Nutrition Information (per serving):

- Calories: 187 kcal
- Protein: 7g
- Carbohydrates: 22g
- Dietary Fiber: 6g
- Sugars: 3g
- Fat: 8g
- Saturated Fat: 1g
- Cholesterol: 0mg
- Sodium: 246mg
- Potassium: 196mg

KALAMATA OLIVE TAPENADE

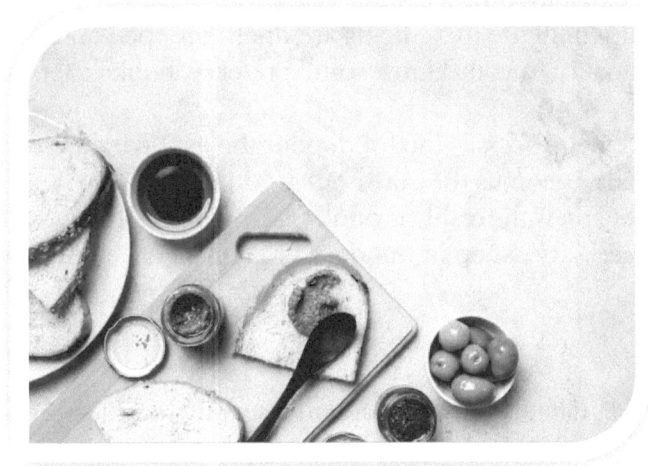

Prep Time: 10 minutes. **Servings:** About 1 cup

Ingredients:

- 1 cup pitted Kalamata olives
- 2 cloves garlic, minced
- 2 tablespoons capers, drained
- 2 tablespoons fresh parsley, chopped
- 2 teaspoons fresh lemon juice
- 2 tablespoons extra-virgin olive oil
- Freshly ground black pepper, to taste

Instructions:

Prepare the Ingredients:

1. Ensure that the Kalamata olives are pitted.
2. Mince the garlic cloves.
3. Drain the capers.
4. Chop the fresh parsley.

<u>Make the Tapenade:</u>

5. Combine the pitted Kalamata olives, minced garlic, capers, chopped fresh parsley, and lemon juice in a food processor.
6. Pulse the mixture until the ingredients are finely chopped and well combined. You can adjust the texture to your liking; some prefer a chunkier tapenade, while others like it smoother.
7. While the machine processes the food, pour the extra-virgin olive oil little by little until the tapenade becomes the consistency you want.
8. Season the tapenade with freshly ground black pepper. Try the food and add more seasonings if necessary. Keep in mind that Kalamata olives and capers already have salt in them.

<u>Serve:</u>

9. Transfer the Kalamata Olive Tapenade to a serving bowl.
10. You can serve it as a dip with toasted baguette slices, crackers, or vegetable sticks. It also makes a delicious sandwich spread or a topping for grilled meats or fish.

Nutrition Information (per serving - 1 tablespoon):

- Calories: 29 kcal
- Protein: 0g
- Carbohydrates: 1g
- Dietary Fiber: 1g
- Sugars: 0g
- Fat: 3g
- Saturated Fat: 0g
- Cholesterol: 0mg
- Sodium: 235mg
- Potassium: 14mg

ALMOND 'YOU MUST BE NUTS' CRACKERS

Prep Time: 10 minutes | **Baking Time:** 15-20 minutes | **Servings:** About 24 crackers

Ingredients:

- 1 cup almond flour
- 1/4 cup flaxseed meal
- 1/4 cup sesame seeds
- 1/4 teaspoon salt
- 1/4 teaspoon garlic powder (optional)
- 1/4 teaspoon onion powder (optional)
- 1/4 cup water
- 1 tablespoon extra-virgin olive oil

Instructions:

Preheat the Oven:

1. Preheat your oven to 325°F (160°C). Line a baking sheet with parchment paper.

Mix Dry Ingredients:

2. In a mixing bowl, combine almond flour, flaxseed meal, sesame seeds, salt, garlic powder (if using), and onion powder (if using). Mix well to combine.

Add Wet Ingredients:

3. Add water and extra-virgin olive oil to the dry ingredients. Stir until a dough forms. You may need to use your hands to knead the dough briefly to ensure it comes together.

Roll Out the Dough:

4. Put the dough in the middle of two sheets of parchment paper. Using a rolling pin, roll the dough out to your desired thickness. For crispy crackers, aim for about 1/8-inch thick. Thinner crackers will be crispier.

Cut Into Shapes:

5. Remove the top sheet of parchment paper. Cut the rolled-out dough into desired cracker shapes using a knife or pizza cutter. You can make squares and rectangles or use cookie cutters for fun shapes.

Transfer to Baking Sheet:

6. Carefully transfer the cut crackers onto the prepared baking sheet. Leave a little space between each cracker, but they don't spread much during baking.

Bake:

7. Put the baking sheet with the crackers in the oven and cook them for about 15 to 20 minutes | until they turn golden brown and crispy. Keep a close eye on them; they can quickly go from perfectly crisp to overdone.

Cool and Serve:

8. Remove the crackers from the oven and let them cool on a metal rack.
9. Once cool, your Almond 'You Must Be Nuts' Crackers are ready to enjoy as a snack or with your favorite dips and spreads.

Nutrition Information (per serving - 2 crackers):

- Calories: 70 kcal
- Protein: 2g
- Carbohydrates: 3g
- Dietary Fiber: 1g
- Sugars: 0g
- Fat: 6g
- Saturated Fat: 0g

- Cholesterol: 0mg
- Sodium: 39mg
- Potassium: 24mg

SPANAKOPITA

Prep Time: 30 minutes | **Cooking Time:** 45 minutes | **Servings:** 6-8

Ingredients:

- 1 pound (450g) fresh spinach, washed and chopped (or you can use frozen spinach, thawed and drained)
- 1 cup crumbled feta cheese
- 1/2 cup ricotta cheese
- 1/2 cup grated Parmesan cheese
- 1 small onion, finely chopped
- 2 cloves garlic, minced
- 2 tablespoons olive oil
- 3 large eggs, beaten
- 1/4 cup fresh dill, chopped (or 1 tablespoon dried dill)
- 1/4 cup fresh parsley, chopped
- Salt and pepper to taste
- 1 package phyllo pastry sheets (16 ounces), thawed
- 1/2 cup unsalted butter, melted

Instructions:

<u>Prepare the Spinach Mixture:</u>

1. Heat olive oil in a large skillet over medium heat. Add the chopped onion and garlic, and sauté until they become translucent.
2. Put the chopped spinach into the pan and cook until it becomes soft and any extra water dries up. Allow the cooked spinach mixture to cool.
3. Mix the cooled spinach mixture, crumbled feta cheese, ricotta cheese, grated Parmesan cheese, beaten eggs, fresh dill, parsley, salt, and pepper in a big bowl. Mix well to combine.

<u>Assemble the Spanakopita:</u>

4. Preheat your oven to 350°F (175°C).
5. Take out the thawed phyllo pastry sheets and spread them out. Put a wet kitchen towel on top of them so they don't become dry.
6. Take one sheet of phyllo pastry and brush it lightly with melted butter. Place another sheet on top and repeat the process until you have a stack of about 6 sheets.
7. Cut the stacked phyllo sheets into long strips approximately 3 inches wide.
8. Put a spoonful of the spinach and cheese mixture at the bottom of each strip.
9. Fold the phyllo pastry over the filling, creating a triangle-shaped parcel. Continue folding in a triangle shape until you reach the end of the strip.
10. Put the completed spanakopita triangles on a baking sheet with parchment paper, with the folded side facing down. Brush the tops with more melted butter.

<u>Bake:</u>

11. Bake in the oven for 40-45 minutes | until the spanakopita triangles are golden brown and crispy.

<u>Serve:</u>

12. Remove from the oven and let cool for a few minutes | before serving. Spanakopita can be enjoyed either warm or at a normal temperature.

Nutrition Information (per serving - 1 piece, based on 8 servings):

- Calories: 328 kcal
- Protein: 11g
- Carbohydrates: 14g
- Dietary Fiber: 2g
- Sugars: 1g

- Fat: 26g
- Saturated Fat: 13g
- Cholesterol: 121mg
- Sodium: 567mg
- Potassium: 429mg

FIGS STUFFED WITH GOAT CHEESE AND ALMONDS

Prep Time: 15 minutes | **Cooking Time:** 0 minutes | (no cooking required) **Servings:** 12 stuffed figs

Ingredients:

- 12 fresh figs
- 4 ounces (113g) goat cheese
- 1/4 cup almonds, chopped
- 2 tablespoons honey for drizzling
- Fresh thyme leaves, for garnish (optional)

Instructions:

Prepare the Figs:

1. Wash and dry the fresh figs. Slice off the top stem of each fig and make a small "X" cut on the top, about halfway down. Be careful not to cut all the way through.

Make the Goat Cheese Filling:

2. Combine in a bowl the goat cheese and chopped almonds. Mix them until well combined.

Fill the Figs:

3. Take a small spoonful of the goat cheese and almond mixture and stuff it into the center of each fig, gently pressing down to secure the filling.

Drizzle with Honey:

4. Place the stuffed figs on a plate for serving. Drizzle honey over the top of each stuffed fig. The sweetness of the honey pairs beautifully with the tangy goat cheese and the natural sweetness of the figs.

Garnish:

5. Sprinkle fresh thyme leaves on the figs to add a more delicious taste and smell.

Serve:

6. Serve the Figs Stuffed With Goat Cheese and Almonds as an appetizer, a cheese platter addition, or a delightful dessert. They are best enjoyed fresh.

Nutrition Information (per stuffed fig):

- Calories: 69 kcal
- Protein: 2g
- Carbohydrates: 10g
- Dietary Fiber: 1g
- Sugars: 8g
- Fat: 3g
- Saturated Fat: 2g
- Cholesterol: 5mg
- Sodium: 40mg
- Potassium: 133mg

AVOCADO AND BLACK-EYED PEA SALSA

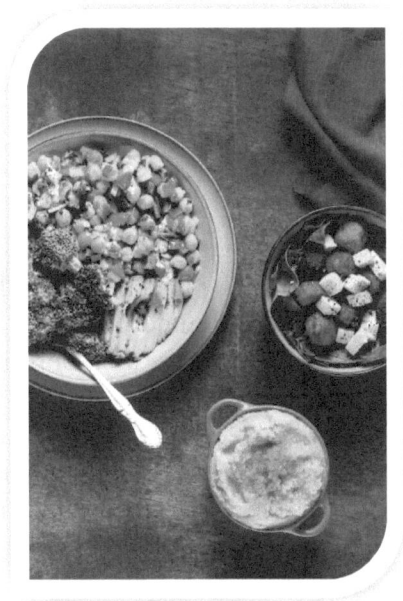

Prep Time: 15 minutes | **Chilling Time:** 30 minutes | (optional) **Servings:** 4-6

Ingredients:

- 1 can (15 ounces) black-eyed peas, drained and rinsed
- 2 ripe avocados, diced
- 1 cup cherry tomatoes, halved
- 1/2 cup red onion, finely chopped
- 1/4 cup fresh cilantro, chopped
- 1 jalapeño pepper, seeds removed and finely chopped (adjust to taste)
- 2 cloves garlic, minced
- Juice of 2 limes
- 2 tablespoons extra-virgin olive oil
- Salt and pepper to taste
- Tortilla chips for serving

Instructions:

<u>Prepare the Ingredients:</u>

1. Drain and rinse the black-eyed peas thoroughly. Let them drain well.
2. Dice the ripe avocados and place them in a mixing bowl. Squeeze some lime juice over them to prevent browning.
3. Halve the cherry tomatoes, finely chop the red onion, chop the fresh cilantro, and mince the garlic cloves.

<u>Make the Salsa:</u>

4. Combine the drained black-eyed peas, diced avocados, halved cherry tomatoes, chopped red onion, fresh cilantro, and minced garlic in a large mixing bowl.
5. Add the finely chopped jalapeño pepper for a bit of heat. Change the amount based on how much spice you like.
6. Drizzle the juice of 2 limes and extra-virgin olive oil over the mixture.
7. Gently mix all the ingredients until they are well combined.
8. Season the salsa with salt and pepper to taste. Be sure to taste and adjust the seasoning as needed.

<u>Chill and Serve:</u>

9. For the best flavor, cover the salsa and refrigerate it for about 30 minutes | to allow the flavors to meld. However, you can also serve it immediately if you can't wait!

<u>Serve:</u>

10. Serve the Avocado and blackyed Eyed Pea Salsa with tortilla chips, fish, or tacos.

Nutrition Information (per serving - 1/6 of the recipe):

- Calories: 209 kcal
- Protein: 6g
- Carbohydrates: 18g
- Dietary Fiber: 7g
- Sugars: 2g
- Fat: 14g
- Saturated Fat: 2g
- Cholesterol: 0mg
- Sodium: 299mg
- Potassium: 516mg

SARDINES WITH SUN-DRIED TOMATOES AND CAPERS

Prep Time: 15 minutes | **Cooking Time:** 10 minutes | **Servings:** 2

Ingredients:

- 4 fresh sardine fillets, scaled and gutted
- 1/4 cup sun-dried tomatoes in oil, drained and chopped
- 2 tablespoons capers, rinsed and drained
- 2 cloves garlic, minced
- 2 tablespoons extra-virgin olive oil
- Juice of 1 lemon
- 1/4 teaspoon red pepper flakes (adjust to taste)
- Salt and black pepper to taste
- Fresh parsley, chopped for garnish (optional)
- Lemon wedges for serving

Instructions:

Prepare the Sardines:

1. If your sardines are whole, wash them with cold water and dry them with paper towels. Carefully fillet them, removing the bones and any innards. You can also ask your fishmonger to fillet them for you.

<u>Make the Sun-Dried Tomato and Caper Sauce:</u>

2. In a small bowl, combine the chopped sun-dried tomatoes, capers, minced garlic, virgin olive oil, lemon juice, red pepper flakes, salt, and black pepper. Mix well to create a flavorful sauce.

<u>Cook the Sardines:</u>

3. Heat a grill or a flat pan with grills on it over medium to high heat. Brush the sardine fillets with a little olive oil to prevent sticking.
4. Grill the sardine fillets for 2-3 minutes | per side or until they are cooked through and have grill marks. The time it takes to cook the fillets may differ depending on their thickness.

<u>Serve:</u>

5. Place the grilled sardines on a serving platter.
6. Spoon the sun-dried tomato and caper sauce over the top of the sardines.
7. Sprinkle some freshly chopped parsley on top, and serve with slices of lemon next to it.

Nutrition Information (per serving - 2 fillets with sauce):

- Calories: 280 kcal
- Protein: 28g
- Carbohydrates: 8g
- Dietary Fiber: 2g
- Sugars: 2g
- Fat: 16g
- Saturated Fat: 3g
- Cholesterol: 77mg
- Sodium: 764mg
- Potassium: 637mg

REAL HUMMUS

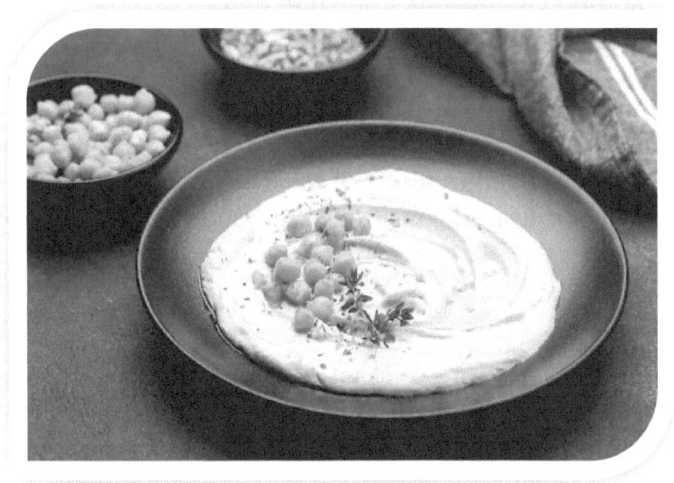

Prep Time: 10 minutes | **Cooking Time:** 0 minutes | **Servings:** About 2 cups

Ingredients:

- 1 can (15 ounces) chickpeas (garbanzo beans), drained and rinsed
- 1/4 cup fresh lemon juice (about 1 large lemon)
- 1/4 cup well-stirred tahini
- 1 small garlic clove, minced
- 2 tablespoons extra-virgin olive oil, plus more for serving
- 1/2 teaspoon ground cumin
- Salt, to taste
- 2 to 3 tablespoons water
- Dash of paprika for garnish (optional)
- Fresh parsley, chopped, for garnish (optional)

Instructions:

Prepare the Chickpeas:

1. Drain and rinse the canned chickpeas thoroughly under cold running water. This helps remove excess salt and the canning liquid.

Blend the Ingredients:

2. In a food processor, combine the chickpeas, fresh lemon juice, well-stirred tahini, minced garlic, ground cumin, and a pinch of salt.
3. Process the mixture for about 20 seconds.
4. Scrape down the sides of the bowl and then process for another 20-30 seconds or until the hummus is well blended and creamy.
5. While the food processor is running, slowly drizzle in the 2 tablespoons of extra-virgin olive oil and 2 to 3 tablespoons of water. Continue to process until the hummus reaches your desired consistency. If it's too thick, add more water, a tablespoon at a time.

Taste and Adjust:

6. Try the hummus and add more spices if it needs more flavor. Add extra salt, lemon juice, or some cumin to match your liking.

Serve:

7. Transfer the hummus to a serving bowl.
8. Drizzle with extra-virgin olive oil and sprinkle with a dash of paprika for color and flavor. You can also garnish with fresh chopped parsley if desired.

Enjoy:

9. Serve your Real Hummus with pita bread, pita chips, fresh vegetables, or as a dip for your favorite Mediterranean dishes.

Nutrition Information (per 2-tablespoon serving):

- Calories: 45 kcal
- Protein: 1g
- Carbohydrates: 2g
- Dietary Fiber: 1g
- Sugars: 0g
- Fat: 4g
- Saturated Fat: 0.5g
- Cholesterol: 0mg
- Sodium: 25mg
- Potassium: 38mg

HONEY-CINNAMON TAHINI SPREAD

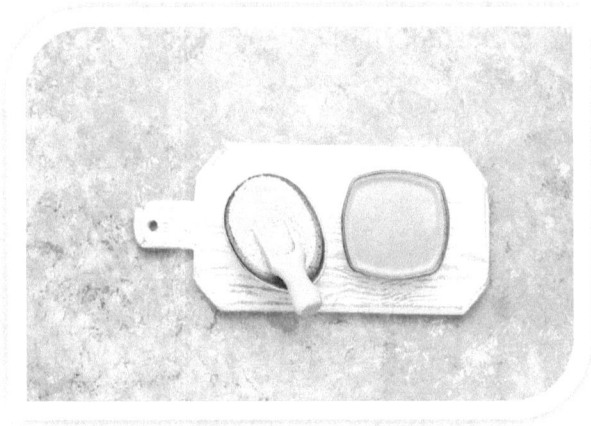

Prep Time: 5 minutes | **Cooking Time:** 0 minutes | **Servings:** About 1 cup

Ingredients:

- 1/2 cup tahini (sesame seed paste)
- 2 tablespoons honey (adjust to taste)
- 1/2 teaspoon ground cinnamon (adjust to taste)
- 1/2 teaspoon pure vanilla extract
- Pinch of salt
- 2-3 tablespoons warm water (optional)

Instructions:

Prepare the Ingredients:

1. Ensure that your tahini is well-stirred before using it. Tahini tends to separate, so mix it thoroughly before measuring.

Make the Honey-Cinnamon Tahini Spread:

2. Combine the tahini, honey, ground cinnamon, pure vanilla extract, and a pinch of salt in a mixing bowl.
3. Stir the ingredients together until they are well combined. The mixture should become creamy and smooth.

4. Taste the spread and adjust the sweetness and cinnamon to your liking. Add more honey if you prefer it sweeter; if you prefer a stronger cinnamon flavor, add more ground cinnamon.
5. If the spread is too thick for your preference, you can thin it out by adding warm water, one tablespoon at a time, until you reach your desired consistency.

Serve:

6. Transfer the Honey-Cinnamon Tahini Spread to a jar or airtight container.

Enjoy:

7. Use this delicious spread as a topping for toast, pancakes, waffles, yogurt, or oatmeal. It can also be drizzled over fresh fruit or used as a dip for apple slices and carrot sticks.

Nutrition Information (per 1-tablespoon serving):

- Calories: 60 kcal
- Protein: 1g
- Carbohydrates: 4g
- Dietary Fiber: 0g
- Sugars: 3g
- Fat: 5g
- Saturated Fat: 1g
- Cholesterol: 0mg
- Sodium: 10mg
- Potassium: 35mg

CHAPTER 6: SWEET MEDITERRANEAN TREATS

HONEY AND YOGURT PARFAIT

Prep Time: 10 minutes | **Cooking Time:** 0 minutes | **Servings:** 2

Ingredients:

- 2 cups Greek yogurt (full-fat or low-fat)
- 4 tablespoons honey (adjust to taste)
- 1 cup fresh berries (such as strawberries, blueberries, or raspberries)
- 1/4 cup granola
- 1/4 teaspoon vanilla extract (optional)
- Fresh mint leaves for garnish (optional)

Instructions:

Prepare the Yogurt Mixture:

1. In a bowl, mix the Greek yogurt and honey. If you want, you can put a little bit of vanilla extract to make it taste better.
2. Stir the yogurt and honey mixture until well combined. Try the taste; add more honey if it's not sweet enough.

Assemble the Parfait:

3. Choose two serving glasses or bowls.
4. Begin by spooning a layer of the honey-sweetened yogurt into the bottom of each glass.
5. Put some fresh berries on top of the yogurt.
6. Sprinkle a layer of granola over the berries.
7. Keep adding layers until the glasses are full. Finally, put a scoop of yogurt on top.

Garnish and Serve:

8. Garnish the parfaits with fresh mint leaves if desired.
9. Drizzle a little extra honey over the top for an extra touch of sweetness.

Enjoy:

10. Serve your Honey and Yogurt Parfait immediately as a delicious and nutritious breakfast or snack.

Nutrition Information (per serving):

- Calories: 280 kcal
- Protein: 15g
- Carbohydrates: 46g
- Dietary Fiber: 4g
- Sugars: 36g
- Fat: 5g
- Saturated Fat: 1g
- Cholesterol: 10mg
- Sodium: 40mg
- Potassium: 290mg

FIG AND WALNUT BITES

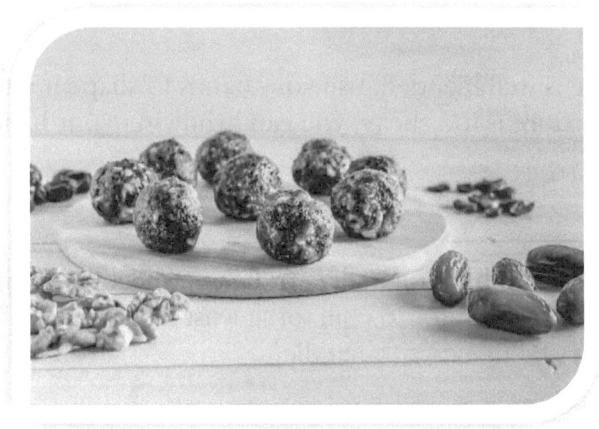

Prep Time: 15 minutes | **Chilling Time:** 30 minutes | **Servings:** Approximately 12 bites

Ingredients:

- 1 cup dried figs, stems removed
- 1/2 cup walnuts
- 1/4 cup unsweetened shredded coconut
- 1 tablespoon honey (adjust to taste)
- 1/2 teaspoon ground cinnamon
- Pinch of salt
- Additional shredded coconut for rolling (optional)

Instructions:

Prepare the Ingredients:

1. Start by removing the stems from the dried figs if they have them.

Blend the Ingredients:

2. Combine the dried figs, walnuts, unsweetened shredded coconut, honey, ground cinnamon, and a pinch of salt in a food processor.

3. Process the mixture until it reaches a sticky, crumbly texture. You might have to pause and clean the edges of the food processor a couple of times to ensure everything mixes properly.

Form the Bites:

4. Once the mixture is well blended, use your hands to shape it into bite-sized balls or squares. If the mixture is too sticky, you can lightly wet your hands to make it easier to work.

Chill:

5. Place the fig and walnut bites on a plate or baking sheet lined with parchment paper.
6. Put the bites in the refrigerator to chill for at least 30 minutes. Chilling helps them firm up and makes them easier to handle.

Optional: Coat with Coconut:

7. If you want, sprinkle more shredded coconut on the cold bites to make them taste and feel even better.

Serve:

8. Transfer the Fig and Walnut Bites to a serving plate or container.

Enjoy:

9. These Fig and Walnut Bites make a nutritious and naturally sweet snack. They're great for satisfying your craving for something sweet and helping with digestion and healthy fats from the figs and walnuts.

Nutrition Information (per bite):

- Calories: 70 kcal
- Protein: 1g
- Carbohydrates: 10g
- Dietary Fiber: 2g
- Sugars: 7g
- Fat: 3g
- Saturated Fat: 0.5g
- Cholesterol: 0mg
- Sodium: 5mg
- Potassium: 100mg

CHOCOLATE CHIA PUDDING

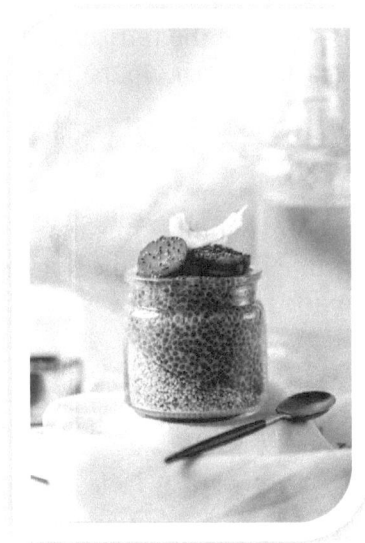

Prep Time: 5 minutes | **Chilling Time:** 2-4 hours (or overnight) **Servings:** 2

Ingredients:

- 1/4 cup chia seeds
- 2 tablespoons unsweetened cocoa powder
- 2 tablespoons maple syrup or honey (adjust to taste)
- 1/2 teaspoon vanilla extract
- 1 1/2 cups unsweetened almond milk (or any milk of your choice)
- Fresh berries, sliced bananas, or chopped nuts for topping (optional)

Instructions:

Mix the Base:

1. In a mixing bowl, combine the chia seeds and unsweetened cocoa powder.
2. Add the maple syrup (or honey) and vanilla extract to the bowl.
3. Gradually pour in the unsweetened almond milk while whisking continuously to prevent clumps. Continue to whisk until all the ingredients are well combined.

4. Cover the bowl with plastic wrap or transfer the mixture to individual serving glasses or jars.
5. Place the Chocolate Chia Pudding in the refrigerator to chill for at least 2-4 hours or overnight. This helps the chia seeds soak up the liquid and turn into a pudding-like texture.

Serve:

6. When you are about to serve the pudding, mix it well. If the mixture is too thick, pour in more almond milk until it becomes the thickness you want.
7. Divide the pudding into serving glasses or bowls.

Top and Enjoy:

8. Garnish the Chocolate Chia Pudding with fresh berries, sliced bananas, or any other toppings you prefer.

Nutrition Information (per serving, without toppings):

- Calories: 160 kcal
- Protein: 4g
- Carbohydrates: 21g
- Dietary Fiber: 10g
- Sugars: 6g
- Fat: 7g
- Saturated Fat: 0.5g
- Cholesterol: 0mg
- Sodium: 140mg
- Potassium: 180mg

MIXED BERRY CRISP

Prep Time: 15 minutes | **Baking Time:** 30-35 minutes | **Servings:** 6

Ingredients:

<u>For the Filling:</u>

- 4 cups mixed berries (strawberries, blueberries, raspberries, and blackberries)
- 1/4 cup granulated sugar
- 1 tablespoon cornstarch
- 1 tablespoon lemon juice
- 1/2 teaspoon vanilla extract

<u>For the Topping:</u>

- 1 cup old-fashioned rolled oats
- 1/2 cup all-purpose flour
- 1/4 cup brown sugar (packed)
- 1/4 cup granulated sugar
- 1/2 teaspoon ground cinnamon
- Pinch of salt
- 1/2 cup unsalted butter (cold and cubed)

Instructions:

<u>Preheat the Oven:</u>

1. Preheat your oven to 350°F (175°C).

<u>Prepare the Filling:</u>

2. Combine the mixed berries, granulated sugar, cornstarch, lemon juice, and vanilla extract in a large bowl. Toss to coat the berries evenly.

<u>Assemble the Crisp:</u>

3. Transfer the berry mixture to a 9x9-inch (23x23 cm) baking dish or a similar-sized ovenproof dish.

<u>Prepare the Topping:</u>

4. Combine the rolled oats, all-purpose flour, brown sugar, granulated sugar, ground cinnamon, and a pinch of salt in a separate bowl.
5. Put the cold into small square pieces and unsalted butter into the dry mixture. You can use a tool or your hands to mix the butter into the dry ingredients until it looks like small crumbs and feels like coarse grains.

<u>Top the Berries:</u>

6. Sprinkle the oat and sugar mixture evenly over the berry filling in the baking dish.

<u>Bake:</u>

7. Put the baking dish in the oven and cook for 30 to 35 minutes | until the topping is golden and the berry filling is bubbling.

<u>Serve:</u>

8. Remove the Mixed Berry Crisp from the oven and let it cool slightly before serving.

<u>Enjoy:</u>

9. You can eat it warm or with a scoop of vanilla ice cream or whipped cream.

Nutrition Information (per serving):

- Calories: 300 kcal
- Protein: 3g
- Carbohydrates: 48g

- Dietary Fiber: 6g
- Sugars: 27g
- Fat: 11g
- Saturated Fat: 6g
- Cholesterol: 25mg
- Sodium: 10mg
- Potassium: 220mg

CINNAMON SPICED PEACHES WITH HONEY & GREEK YOGURT

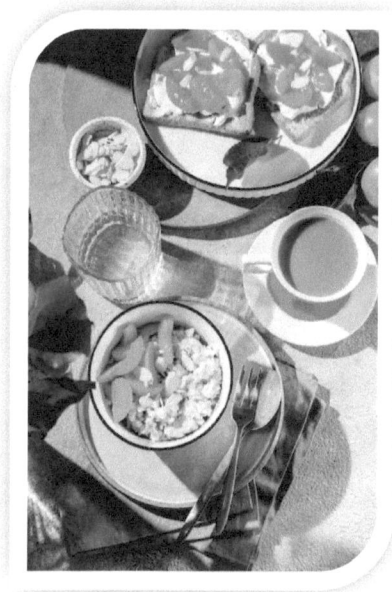

Prep Time: 10 minutes | **Cooking Time:** 10 minutes | **Servings:** 4

Ingredients:

For the Cinnamon Spiced Peaches:

- 4 ripe peaches, peeled, pitted, and sliced
- 2 tablespoons unsalted butter
- 2 tablespoons honey
- 1 teaspoon ground cinnamon
- 1/4 teaspoon vanilla extract
- Pinch of salt

For Serving:

- Greek yogurt (or yogurt of your choice)
- Additional honey for drizzling

- Chopped nuts (such as almonds or walnuts) for garnish (optional)

Instructions:

Prepare the Peaches:

1. Begin by peeling, pitting, and slicing the ripe peaches. Set them aside.

Cook the cinnamon-spiced peaches:

2. In a large skillet, melt the unsalted butter over medium heat.
3. Add the sliced peaches to the skillet.
4. Pour the honey over the peaches and sprinkle with cinnamon powder.
5. Add the vanilla extract and a pinch of salt to the skillet.
6. Gently stir the peaches to coat them evenly with the butter, honey, and spices.
7. Cook the peaches for about 5-7 minutes | until they are tender and the sauce has thickened slightly. Stir occasionally.

Serve:

8. Divide the warm Cinnamon Spiced Peaches among serving bowls.

Add Greek Yogurt:

9. Spoon a generous dollop of Greek yogurt (or yogurt of your choice) on top of the warm peaches.

Drizzle with Honey:

10. Drizzle a bit more honey over the yogurt for added sweetness.

Garnish:

11. If desired, garnish with chopped nuts, such as almonds or walnuts.

Enjoy:

12. Serve immediately as a warm and comforting dessert or a delightful breakfast.

Nutrition Information (per serving):
- Calories: 190 kcal
- Protein: 4g
- Carbohydrates: 32g
- Dietary Fiber: 3g

- Sugars: 28g
- Fat: 7g
- Saturated Fat: 4g
- Cholesterol: 20mg
- Sodium: 40mg
- Potassium: 360mg

GRILLED PINEAPPLE WITH WHIPPED GREEK YOGURT AND RUM SAUCE

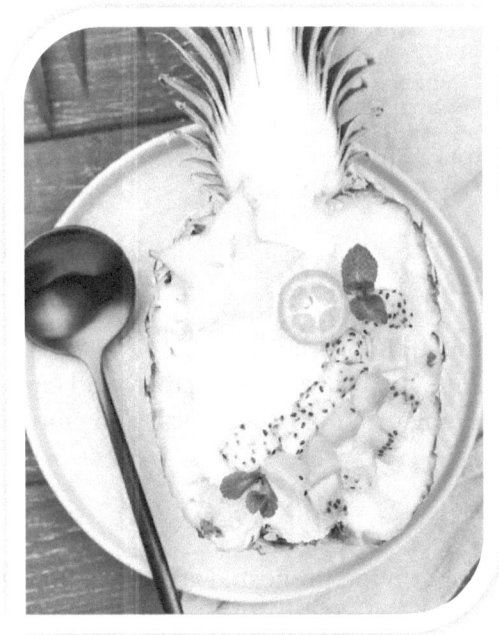

Prep Time: 15 minutes | **Grilling Time:** 6-8 minutes | **Servings:** 4

Ingredients:

For the Grilled Pineapple:

- 1 pineapple, peeled, cored, and sliced into rings
- 2 tablespoons brown sugar
- 1 teaspoon ground cinnamon

For the Whipped Greek Yogurt:

- 1 cup Greek yogurt
- 2 tablespoons honey
- 1 teaspoon vanilla extract

For the Rum Sauce:

- 2 tablespoons unsalted butter
- 2 tablespoons dark rum
- 2 tablespoons brown sugar

For Garnish:

- Fresh mint leaves
- Shredded coconut (optional)

Instructions:

Prepare the Grilled Pineapple:

1. Preheat your grill to medium-high heat.
2. In a small bowl, combine the brown sugar and ground cinnamon.
3. Brush each pineapple ring with the brown sugar and cinnamon mixture on both sides.

Grill the Pineapple:

4. Place the pineapple rings on the preheated grill. Grill for 3-4 minutes | on each side until grill marks appear and the pineapple is slightly caramelized.
5. Take the pineapple off the grill and put it to the side.

Prepare the Whipped Greek Yogurt:

6. Combine the Greek yogurt, honey, and vanilla extract separately. Mix until the mixture becomes smooth and creamy.

Prepare the Rum Sauce:

7. Heat the butter in a small saucepan until it becomes liquid.
8. Mix the dark rum and brown sugar with the melted butter. Keep stirring the sauce until the sugar is completely mixed in and the sauce gets a little thicker.
9. Remove the rum sauce from the heat.

Serve:

10. Place a grilled pineapple ring on each serving plate.
11. Top the grilled pineapple with a generous dollop of whipped Greek yogurt.
12. Drizzle the rum sauce over the yogurt and pineapple.

Garnish:

13. If you want, add fresh mint leaves and shredded coconut on top.

<u>Enjoy:</u>

14. Serve the Grilled Pineapple with Whipped Greek Yogurt and Rum Sauce as a delightful dessert or a tropical treat.

Nutrition Information (per serving):

- Calories: 210 kcal
- Protein: 4g
- Carbohydrates: 35g
- Dietary Fiber: 3g
- Sugars: 26g
- Fat: 6g
- Saturated Fat: 4g
- Cholesterol: 15mg
- Sodium: 30mg
- Potassium: 290mg

DAIRY-FREE BANANA WALNUT ICE CREAM

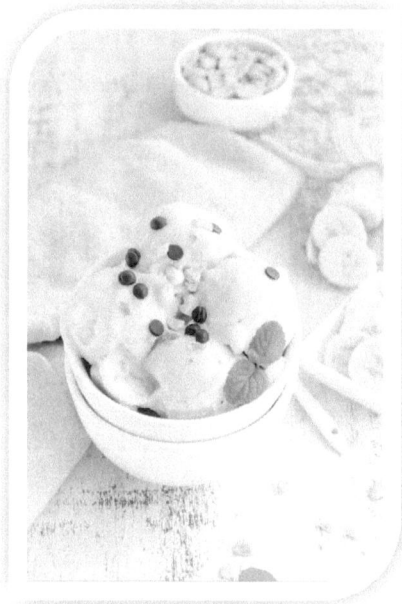

Prep Time: 10 minutes | Freezing Time: 4-6 hours Servings: 4

Ingredients:

- 4 ripe bananas, peeled, sliced, and frozen
- 1/2 cup unsweetened almond milk (or any dairy-free milk of your choice)
- 1 teaspoon vanilla extract
- 1/2 cup chopped walnuts
- 2 tablespoons maple syrup (optional for added sweetness)

Instructions:

Prepare the Frozen Bananas:

1. Cut the ready bananas into coins and put them on a heating sheet lined with material paper. Make, beyond any doubt, the banana cuts are not touching each other.
2. Put the baking sheet with the banana slices in the freezer and leave them there for at least 4 hours or until they become solid.

Blend the Ingredients:

3. Once the banana cuts are solidified, exchange them for a high-speed blender or nourishment processor.
4. Add the unsweetened almond milk, vanilla extract, and maple syrup (if using) to the blender.
5. Mix until the blend is smooth and rich. You may need to stop and scrape down the sides of the blender as needed.

Add the Chopped Walnuts:

6. Add the chopped walnuts to the blender and pulse a few times to incorporate them into the ice cream mixture. Leave some walnuts for garnish, if desired.

Freeze Again:

7. Transfer the banana walnut ice cream mixture into an airtight container.
8. Cover and freeze for 2-3 hours or until the ice cream firms up.

Serve:

9. Scoop the dairy-free Banana Walnut Ice Cream into bowls or cones.

Garnish:

10. Garnish with additional chopped walnuts, if desired.

Enjoy:

11. Serve immediately as a refreshing and guilt-free treat.

Nutrition Information (per serving):

- Calories: 200 kcal
- Protein: 3g
- Carbohydrates: 35g
- Dietary Fiber: 4g
- Sugars: 18g
- Fat: 7g
- Saturated Fat: 1g
- Cholesterol: 0mg
- Sodium: 45mg
- Potassium: 460mg

NO-BAKE PEANUT BUTTER BUCKEYES

Prep Time: 20 minutes | **Chilling Time:** 1 hour **Servings:** About 24 Buckeyes

Ingredients:

For the Peanut Butter Filling:

- 1 cup creamy peanut butter
- 1/2 cup unsalted butter, softened
- 2 cups powdered sugar
- 1 teaspoon vanilla extract
- A pinch of salt

For the Chocolate Coating:

- 2 cups semi-sweet chocolate chips
- 2 tablespoons vegetable shortening or coconut oil

For Decorating:

- 24 toothpicks or wooden skewers

Instructions:

<u>Prepare the Peanut Butter Filling:</u>

1. Combine the softened unsalted butter and creamy peanut butter in a mixing bowl. Mix until well combined.
2. Add the powdered sugar, vanilla extract, and a little salt to the peanut butter mixture. Mix until the mixture is smooth and forms a dough-like consistency.
3. Shape the peanut butter mixture into 1-inch balls (about the size of a walnut) and place them on a baking sheet lined with parchment paper. You should have about 24 peanut butter balls.
4. Insert a toothpick or wooden skewer into each peanut butter ball. Put the heating sheet within the cooler for 30 minutes | to firm up the peanut butter balls.

<u>Prepare the Chocolate Coating:</u>

5. Combine the semi-sweet chocolate chips and vegetable shortening or coconut oil in a microwave-safe bowl.
6. Microwave in 20-30-second intervals, stirring after each interval, until the chocolate becomes smooth and completely melted. Be careful not to overheat the chocolate.

<u>Dip the Peanut Butter Balls:</u>

7. Take out the peanut butter balls from the freezer. Take a toothpick or skewer and put a chocolate coating on each ball. Make sure to leave a little bit of the peanut butter showing at the top so it looks like a buckeye nut.
8. Allow any excess chocolate to drip back into the bowl, and then place the dipped buckeyes back onto the parchment-lined baking sheet.
9. Remove the toothpick or skewer from each buckeye, leaving a small hole at the top.

<u>Chill and Serve:</u>

10. Place the baking sheet with the buckeyes in the refrigerator for about 30 minutes | to set the chocolate.
11. Once the chocolate has set, you can use a toothpick or your finger to fill in the hole left by the toothpick with a small amount of melted chocolate to create the traditional buckeye look.
12. Serve the No-Bake Shelled nut Butter Buckeyes chilled. Store any remains in a waterproof holder within the fridge.

<u>Enjoy:</u>

13. Enjoy these delicious and indulgent peanut butter treats!

Nutrition Information (per serving - 1 buckeye):

- Calories: 180 kcal
- Protein: 2g
- Carbohydrates: 16g
- Dietary Fiber: 1g
- Sugars: 13g
- Fat: 12g
- Saturated Fat: 5g
- Cholesterol: 10mg
- Sodium: 50mg
- Potassium: 100mg

CONCLUSION:
A LIFETIME OF HEALTH AND FLAVOR

As you reach the final pages of "Mediterranean Diet for Beginners," we hope your culinary journey through the Mediterranean has left you inspired, enlightened, and nourished in body and soul. The recipes you've explored are not just a collection of dishes but a gateway to a lifestyle that promises a lifetime of health and flavor.

The Mediterranean diet is more than just a trend; it's a timeless tradition that has stood the test of time. Its enduring popularity is a testament to the harmony it brings to our plates and lives. Throughout this cookbook, we've celebrated the cornerstone principles of this diet: an abundance of fresh fruits and vegetables, whole grains, heart-healthy fats, and lean proteins. We've marveled at the vivid colors and flavors that dance on our taste buds with each bite.

But beyond the delectable recipes, the Mediterranean diet offers many health benefits. It reduces the risk of chronic diseases, promotes cardiovascular health, supports cognitive function, and contributes to longevity. As you've embraced these dishes, you've embraced a path to wellness.

As you conclude your journey through these pages, remember that the Mediterranean diet is not just about the food—it's about savoring life's moments, gathering with loved ones, and nurturing both body and spirit. Whether you're sharing a simple meal with family, hosting a gathering of friends, or enjoying a quiet dinner for two, the Mediterranean way of eating can be your constant companion.

We encourage you to continue exploring the rich tapestry of Mediterranean flavors, experimenting with ingredients, and making these dishes your own. Let this cookbook serve as a foundation for your culinary adventures, and let the Mediterranean diet be a lifelong companion on your path to health and well-being.

May your kitchen always be filled with the aromas of olive oil, herbs, and wholesome ingredients. May your meals be a celebration of life and vitality. May your journey through the Mediterranean diet be a source of lifelong health and flavor.

Thank you for joining us on this flavorful voyage. May your days be filled with good health, joy, and the irresistible flavors of the Mediterranean.

Bon appétit and cheers to a lifetime of health and flavor!

Your,
Anna Roux

Made in United States
Troutdale, OR
05/18/2024